The

Year

of the

Poet VI

October 2019

The Poetry Posse

inner child press, ltd.

The Poetry Posse 2019

Gail Weston Shazor

Shareef Abdur Rasheed

Teresa E. Gallion

hülya n. yılmaz

Kimberly Burnham

Tzemin Ition Tsai

Elizabeth Esguerra Castillo

Jackie Davis Allen

Joe Paire

Caroline 'Ceri' Nazareno

Ashok K. Bhargava

Alicja Maria Kuberska

Swapna Behera

Albert 'Infinite' Carrasco

Eliza Segiet

William S. Peters, Sr.

The Year of the Poet VI
October 2019 Edition

The Poetry Posse

1st Edition : 2019

Publisher Information

1st Edition : Inner Child Press
intouch@innerchildpress.com
www.innerchildpress.com

$ 12.99

WHAT WOULD LIFE BE WITHOUT A LITTLE POETRY?

Dedication

This Book is dedicated to

Poetry . . .

The Poetry Posse

past, present & future

our Patrons and Readers

the Spirit of our Everlasting Muse

&

the Power of the Pen

to effectuate change!

In the darkness of my life
I heard the music
I danced . . .
and the Light appeared
and I dance

Janet P. Caldwell

Table of Contents

The Poetry Posse

Table of Contents . . . *continued*

October's Featured Poets   107

Foreword

North Africa and the Nile Valley

One of the most important pieces of real estate on earth and extremely large at that is North Africa and the Nile Valley. Historically it is hard to find to many other areas of the world that is as historically significant. That being said the degree of historical and even contemporary significance is off the charts. This is a forward of a poetry anthology published monthly with the theme for October 2019 North Africa and the Nile Valley not volume one of a double digit set of very thick books concerning this area of the globe. After establishing that fact let me at least attempt to indulge you in a condensed overview to touch on a few facts regarding this extremely unique, diverse area of the world.

Firstly the group of talented poets using their ample artful skills to encapsulate this theme in their work is the ' Poetry Posse ', who are as diverse as the make-up of this theme and who even include poets from this region. The Posse is featured monthly in the publication ' The Year of The Poet/Poetry Posse published monthly by Inner Child Press. http://www.innerchildpress.com, now through more then two thirds through the sixth year of publication.

The most popular opinions is what constitutes North Africa is from the west Atlantic shores of Mauritania to Egypt's Suez Canal and Red Sea in the east. Another is that what is North Africa is from the northwest of Africa going east, Morocco, Algeria, Tunisia, Libya, Egypt and Sudan the 6 countries that occupy the North of the African continent. In addition, there are several Spanish and Portuguese possessions. Arabic is the major language across the whole of North Africa. In addition, there is Berber language spoken by Berber people along with Arabic. They are mostly in Morocco and Algeria. French is also spoken especially in Morocco and Algeria from the French occupation as well as Spanish to a lesser degree mostly in Morocco. The region was ruled by the Romans approximately from 146BC to 476AD. The Muslim conquest and spread of Islam included the region by 640AD, by 700AD the whole of North Africa was under Muslim domination. The Ottomans ruled the region in the middle ages except Morocco. In the 19th century the Europeans came into the picture and Briton, Spain, France and Italy occupied the whole of North Africa. 1940 to 43 WW2 came to the region known as the famous North African campaign, the allies led by Field Marshal Bernard Montgomery the British commander fought Nazi Germany lead by the " Desert Fox General Erwin Rommel. The Allies won the campaign.

Islam remains the prominent religion to the present all though there are also Jews especially in Morocco as well as Christian Copts in Egypt. There are two natural phenomena that are both unique and the largest on earth that run through North Africa and beyond. One is the Sahara Desert the largest on earth over 4,000 miles long and the Nile River the longest river in the world, over 3,000 miles long. The Nile Valley referred to as the cradle of civilization because of the vital part it plays to enhance agriculture to the lands along its banks that have fertile soil as a result that produce life sustaining crops of a variety of fruits and vegetables that are consumed throughout the world therefore is not just a food source but a enormous contributor to the region's economy. This is only a tease in as far as the vast history and therefore library of information about North Africa and the Nile Valley. Please take time to research some of it. Better yet perhaps you can visit the region and get a close up and personal perspective in real time. Enjoy the poetry and peace and blessings.

Shareef Abdur-Rasheed,
Poetry Posse,
Inner Child Press International

World Healing, World Peace Foundation
human beings for humanity

worldhealingworldpeacefoundation.org

World Healing, World Peace 2020
International Poetry Symposium

Dear Friends & Family . . . Poets, Poetry Lovers & Humanitarians

We are so excited at ICPI, Inner Child Press International, as we have begun to mobilize for the upcoming epic event of the 'World Healing, World Peace 2020 Poetry Symposium'. Our plans are set for April of 2020. This event will be held in Atlantic City, New Jersey.

We are now collecting names, emails and telephone numbers for all potential resources that can make this event a highly successful, and one of significance that will have a resounding effect on our world and humanity at large. We are also looking for volunteers who can assist us in many areas of facilitation in the planning, staging and execution phases. Going forward, we will be speaking with the business, government, foundation and the private sectors for funding, sponsorship and suitable venues. So, if you know anything, or know someone, we welcome your input and insights.

We will begin shortly to put together our international guest list.

Communicate with us via our email at :

worldhealingworldpeace@gmail.com

or

whwpfoundation@gmail.com

Visit the Web Site(s) :

worldhealingworldpeacepoetry.com

worldhealingworldpeacefoundation.org

World Healing, World Peace 2020 Anthology is now open for submissions.

Submit to :

worldhealingworldpeace@gmail.com

Please share this information

Thank You

Inner Child Press International
'building bridges of cultural understanding'

www.innerchildpress.com

Preface

Dear Family and Friends,

Yes I am excited? This year we have aligned our vision with that of UNESCO as it honors and acknowledges a variety of Global Indigenous cultures. We are now in our sixth year of publication. As are on our way to hitting another milestone. Needless to say, I am elated. Our initial vision was to just perform at this level for the year of 2014. Since that time we have had the blessed opportunity to include many other wonderful word artists and storytellers in the Poetry Posse from lands, cultures and persuasions all over the world. We have featured hundreds of additional poets, thereby introducing their poetic offerings to our vast global readership.

In keeping with our effort and vision to expand the awareness of poets from all walks by making this offerings accessible, we at Inner Child Press International will continue to make every volume a FREE Download. The books are also available for purchase at the affordable cost of $7.00 per volume.

In the previous years, our monthly themes were Flowers, Birds, Gemstones, Trees and Past Cultures. This year we have elected to continue the

Cultural theme. In each month's volume you will have the opportunity to not only read at least one poem themed by our Poetry Posse members about such culture, but we have included a few words about the culture in our prologue. The reasoning behind this is that now our poetry has the opportunity to be educational for not only the reader, but we poets as well. We hope you find the poetic offerings insightful as we use our poetic form to relay to you what we too have learned through our research in making our offering available to you, our readership.

In closing, we would like to thank you for being an integral part of our amazing journey.

Enjoy our amazing featured poets . . . they are amazing!

Building Cultural Bridges of Understanding . . .

Bless Up . . . From the home in our hearts to yours

Bill

The Poetry Posse
Inner Child Press Ineternational

PS
Do Not forget about the World Healing, World
Peace Poetry effort.

Available here

www.worldhealingworldpeacepoetry.com

**For Free Downloads of Previous Issues of
The Year of the Poet**

www.innerchildpress.com/the-year-of-the-poet

poetry is . . .

The Nile Valley

The Nile Valley . . . . thought by most to be the birthplace of civilization. The lore of this area of our world is steeped in rich ancient history. This includes the conquest of the indigenous Nubian cultures and those which migrated north to implant and thus leave behind a vibrantly rich heritage in the sciences, agriculture, education, literature, architecture but to name a few. For more information on the vast and extensive information available go to :

https://en.wikipedia.org/wiki/Nile_Valley_Civiliza tions

Poets . . .
sowing seeds in the
Conscious Garden of Life,
that those who have yet to come
may enjoy the Flowers.

Poets, Writers . . . know that we are the enchanting magicians that nourishes the seeds of dreams and thoughts . . . it is our words that entice the hearts and minds of others to believe there is something grand about the possibilities that life has to offer and our words tease it forth into action . . . for you are the Poet, the Writer to whom the Gift of Words has been entrusted . . .

~ wsp

Coming
April 2020

The
World Healing, World Peace
International Poetry Symposium

Stay Tuned

for more information

intouch@innerchildpress.com

'building bridges of cultural understanding'

www.innerchildpress.com

Poetry succeeds where instruction fails.

~ wsp

I Fly because ... said the Dreamer to the world. I Can

www.iamjustbill.com

Gail
Weston
Shazor

This is a creative promise ~ my pen will speak to and for the world. Enamored with letters and respectful of their power, I have been writing for most of my life. A mother, daughter, sister and grandmother I give what I have been given, greatfilledly.

Author of . . .

"An Overstanding of an Imperfect Love"
&
Notes from the Blue Roof

Lies My Grandfathers Told Me

available at Inner Child Press.

www.facebook.com/gailwestonshazor
www.innerchildpress.com/gail-weston-shazor
navypoet1@gmail.com

She Is

Spicy tomato apple reds
And cool greens
Bronzes and golds
With blues in between
Black and white and
Earth strong browns
This is the color of a queen
Her lips purse into a small knowing
As the music sings her blues
This is her vibration
Mother sun and daughter moon
Rock that baby bye
In the turning of life
We are birthing colors
In the consciousness of drums
A silvery metallicism of winds
She holds her belly round
And the water moves
Clasping hands of power
The women exchange graces
Laying open palms on this planet
They trace the lines at the joinings
Blessing the ungrown spaces
Waiting to be filled
With the prayers of ancestors
And the wishes of the unborn
Carambola greens
Trust in the rising of each day
Reaching into backward facing footsteps
Sankofa
She is both the future and the past
In eucharistic sanctuary and
With the fire of a flamboyant
She is life

Poet

I switched somewhere this season
From a sharer sharing
To a writer writing
Daily I find both my hands
Full of ink
And in the midst of
Trying to empty them
I no longer have
The allowness required
To grasp hold of new things
The thought of this tires me
And I pray to be tucked
Away
Hidden away
Clefted away
So that I may rest away
For just a spell
Or even longer

The binoculariness of life
Bring things closer
That perhaps should be left
To dreams
And I awaken slowly
To a reality
Far harsher than even I will admit
Has taken me away from center
The place that I need to be
To share my life with you
The thought of this tires me

So I pray
Because even He knew
This would happen
And like every good father

He prepared a place for me to go
So that I might again
Become whole
Become filled
Become purposed
For he gives me my voice
In this season of dormancy
When cleansing clarity
Blankets both the hearer
And the speaker

We collect the pieces of
Our mental selves close
Sorting and weighing the particulates
Of our past lives
Choosing the best wheat
To create a foundation
From which to grow
Discarding thorns of lies
Thistles of unkindness
Tares that mimic Holiness
In its truest form
That which we call righteous
That which should be us
And although our lives may be soiled
We bring them to be washed
Bring them to be made
Repaired

And the thought of this
Tires me
For even in this season
There is work to be done
So I call out to He
Than can equip me
And while I await my turn
I will close my eyes

Fold my hands
Relax my mind
Move everything away from me
That may hinder this respite

Swing low, sweet Chariot
I will gladly alight
When you draw near
For I know there is peace
Within the bower
Because I have been in your arms
Before
And just like today
I am waiting on my season
To change

In the Valley of Kings
(Nonet)

A
Dappled
Light shone forth
Along rivers
Among golden sands
Here we sit among you
Majesties you selected
To be the unified voices
As you speak, we speak, with ancestors

Alicja Maria Kuberska

Alicja Maria Kuberska – awarded Polish poetess, novelist, journalist, editor. She was born in 1960, in Świebodzin, Poland. She now lives in Inowrocław, Poland.

In 2011 she published her first volume of poems entitled: "The Glass Reality". Her second volume "Analysis of Feelings", was published in 2012. The third collection "Moments" was published in English in 2014, both in Poland and in the USA. In 2014, she also published the novel - "Virtual roses" and volume of poems "On the border of dream". Next year her volume entitled "Girl in the Mirror" was published in the UK and "Love me" , " (Not)my poem" in the USA. In 2015 she also edited anthology entitled "The Other Side of the Screen".

In 2016 she edited two volumes: "Taste of Love" (USA), "Thief of Dreams" (Poland) and international anthology entitled " Love is like Air" (USA). In 2017 she published volume entitled "View from the window" (Poland). She also edits series of anthologies entitled "Metaphor of Contemporary" (Poland)

Her poems have been published in numerous anthologies and magazines in Poland, the USA, the UK, Albania, Belgium, Chile, Spain, Israel, Canada, India, Italy, Uzbekistan, Czech Republic, South Korea and Australia. She was a featured poet of New Mirage Journal (USA) in the summer of 2011.

Alicja Kuberska is a member of the Polish Writers Associations in Warsaw, Poland and IWA Bogdani, Albania. She is also a member of directors' board of Soflay Literature Foundation.

Ancient Egypt

Can you not marvel at the pyramids
And not look into the stone eyes of Sphinx?

 Rosetta stone, like a magic key,
 Opened the door to the lost world
Silent for centuries hieroglyphs spoke again
- Inscriptions carved on the temple walls
Began to praise the old gods and rulers.
The memory of the pharaohs returned
And saint hymns soared to the heaven
The gods regained their former glory and power
Humble papyri described days of common people

There is not much left of the old empire
Found objects and words are resting
Behind the glass of museum showcases

Colorful sarcophagi hide mummies- their Ka
The souls -Ba roam the vast desert

Sonnets to Laura in the museum of antiquities

They wanted to live forever-among gods, equal to gods.
They ordered their names incised in the stone of stelas,
So they would endure enchanted in the hieroglyphs-
Immune to rain and wind.

They took necessary and valuable things on their last journey.
Carefully prepared, they crossed the threshold of eternity.
Dark, gazes, full of surprise, follow me from the sarcophagi.
This is not how they imagined Eden and the meeting with fate.
The Book of the Dead did not mention crowds of sightseers.
Their jewels disappeared in display cases, and thieves' pockets.
Desiccated bodies and ancient linen wrappings,
Remain the only souvenirs of life.

No one knows exactly what she looked like or who she was.
Was her hair flaxen?
She did not know she would become the warm breath of a poem.
He fell in eternal love with her. Life parted them, but not death.
The song of sonnets erected an ephemeral monument,
And bestowed immortality.
The words of the songs remained more legible
Than stone pyramids.

She did not do anything, but exist

Conversion

It is a pity that I cannot buy a new soul.
In supermarkets, there are no special offers
- New Soul! On sale!

The old one is dysfunctional.

It is much easier to have a simple vision of the world.
Keep your feet on the ground and don't have dreams.

Being greedy protects the heart.
Life has a physical dimension. Ideals hurt.

Gain a prominent place in the rat race,
Dispose of sentiments, tears.

My soul is able to forgive.
It cannot learn to trust again.

It says it does not enter the same river twice.
Unreasonable? Perhaps.
It does not listen to reason.
It pulls away from people

Jackie
Davis
Allen

Jackie Davis Allen

Jackie Davis Allen, otherwise known as Jacqueline D. Allen or Jackie Allen, grew up in the Cumberland Mountains of Appalachia. As the next eldest daughter of a coal miner father and a stay at home mother, she was the first in her family to attend and graduate from college. Her siblings, in their own right, are accomplished, though she is the only one, to date, that has discovered the gift of writing.

Graduating from Radford University, with a Bachelors of Science degree in Early Education, she taught in both public and private schools. For over a decade she taught private art classes to children both in her home and at a local Art and Framing Shop where she also sold her original soft sculptured Victorian dolls and original christening gowns.

She resides in northern Virginia with her husband, taking much needed get-aways to their mountain home near the Blue Ridge Mountains, a place that evokes memories of days spent growing up in the Appalachian Mountains.

A lover of hats, she has worn many. Following marriage to her college sweetheart, and as wife, mother, grandmother, teacher, tutor, artist, writer, poet and crafter, she is a lover of art and antiques, surrounding herself, always, with books, seeking to learn more.

In 2015 she authored *Looking for Rainbows, Poetry, Prose and Art*, and in 2017, *Dark Side of the Moon*. Both books of mostly narrative poetry were published by Inner Child Press and were edited by hulya n. yilmaz.

http://www.innerchildpress.com/jackie-davis-allen.php
jackiedavisallen.com

Between Here and There

He was but nineteen, a soldier.
Frightened, yet brave. A wife, and a baby
Of necessity, left behind.

Worry, fear, strained the years.
The world-wide, at war.

Who knew what the future might hold?
Always needed, more resources, more men.
Hope rolled the dice against despair.

Marching, fighting against the evil,
Seeking war's end. Midst bullets flying.

Across the desert he, struggled, persevered.
With all his might, praying day and night.
For victory's triumph. Led by General Patton,

The goal, defeat the stench of evil.
Victory more than a dream in the sky.

Thanks be to God, the soldier-man survived.
Triumphly weathered, and worn.
Imagine him, then as young man,

With heart and mind torn to pieces.
Weeping inside. Where no one could see.

The North African campaign. War War II.
To all who served, lived and died
For freedom's cause, we thank you.

We salute you as The Greatest Generation.
May history never forget the sacrifices you made.

Stand-by

How excited I am! Nervous, too.
The take off late, delayed,
And I am stuck in a strange airport.
For hours, it seems.
What am I to do?

I finger my wedding band, anxious,
Wondering why you do not answer the phone.
You were to meet me at Heathrow.
But, here I am, still in New York.
Are you as distraught as I?

The airport limousine deposited me
At the door. It leads to where? I have no idea.
Before me, a hallway. Then stairs.
I am in line, cash in hand.
Breathless. Heart pounding.

A ticket to purchase,
Something called "stand-by".
Only one ticket left. It is in my hand.
I breathe, finally! I am going to be fine.
I dial your number. Again.

Life's Breath

As a writer, I wonder
If ever I am to be quoted.
As having written anything memorable.

Famous quotations are just words

Withstanding the test of time.
So maybe I will never know.
No matter, I will just keep on writing.

As a writer I dream
Of days gone by and wonder
Whatever happened to my dreams.

Will any of them materialize?

Or will they dissapate into the night?
Maybe I will never know, so
I shall just keep on writing!

This one thing I do know.
I must write, it is as important
To me as breath is to life.

It is my motivation to continue on.

For me to live is to write;
And to write is to live.
So, I shall keep on writing.

Tzemin
Ition
Tsai

Dr. Tzemin Ition Tsai (蔡澤民博士) was born in Republic of China, in 1957. He holds a Ph.D. in Chemical Engineering and two Masters of Science in Applied Mathematics and Chemical Engineering. He is a professor at Asia University (Taiwan), editor of "Reading, Writing and Teaching" academic text. He also writes the long-term columns for Chinese Language Monthly in Taiwan.

He is a scholar with a wide range of expertise, while maintaining a common and positive interest in science, engineering and literature member.

He has won many national literary awards. His literary works have been anthologized and published in books, journals, and newspapers in more than 40 countries and have been translated into more than a dozen languages.

The Sea Of Hometown

How many years
Raging waves hit the shore
How many squares and circles can't bear this fierce attack?
Just on the rainy day
Sky cried
Always tempted me to pick up
My arms and legs buried in sand
Did not have even just one time to block
Cobblestones rolled on my naked body
Rolling over and over

It was not me to stir up
These stormy waves
A handful blue
Engulf how many dazzling human worlds
A retrograde vortex
How many unsolvable disputes were involved?
A giant reef that has stood for millions of years
Not far from the shore
I jumped into the sea
Take away all the remaining young youth

Built a home along the coast
Resisted the invasion of evil waves
Let's danced
Shouted
My people
Asked the fishes
Before seawater
was filled with the glass bottle
How to write
An unparalleled poetry?

It was so clear in my heart
Cobblestone
Will not stop me
Threw this poetry into the sea
But will
Accompany me
Watch together
The seawater
Will or will not
Becomes more blue

Words Giving To The Wind

Stripes black alternating with white
Sprinkled in the wall of the half front room
Bamboo curtains was full of tired
Can't stop the wind
Acted wildly

That color
Diluted strong contrast
Who would like to draw
the group of yellow tits in the mountain groves
on the wall?

When the birds
Drumming the tongues under the sunlight
Breeze would definitely be happy
to distribute
those sounds like come from silver bells

That Laid-Back Old Man

Park
Azaleas
And Fences covered with climbing vines
Laid back
come from wrinkles on the face
and also
Let time go slowly

Laid back
Come from crutch on the hand
More
Not allowed time go fleeting

A neatly stacked newspaper on the knees
A heavy cotton overcoat
No room for compromise
Let go of your busy schedule
But need a skill over sixty years
But need a nod of the sunlight which so warm and fine

Hurrying vehicles
Under the acquiescence of aural comprehension
No longer an interference
What can wake him up now
Only left
His grandson's voice
or
His Wife's holding hand
That doesn't require a fine aural comprehension
Just need to feel

Shareef Abdur Rasheed

Shareef Abdur Rasheed

Shareef Abdur-Rasheed, AKA Zakir Flo was born and raised in Brooklyn, New York. His education includes Brooklyn College, Suffolk County Community College and Makkah, Saudi Arabia. He is a Veteran of the Viet Nam era, where in 1969 he reverted to his now reverently embraced Islamic Faith. He is very active in the Islamic community and beyond with his teachings, activism and his humanity.

Shareef's spiritual expression comes through the persona of "Zakir Flo" . Zakir is Arabic for "To remind". Never silent, Shareef Abdur-Rasheed is always dropping science, love, consciousness and signs of the time in rhyme.

Shareef is the Patriarch of the Abdur-Rasheed Family with 9 Children (6 Sons and 3 Daughters) and 41 Grandchildren (24 Boys and 17 Girls).

For more information about Shareef, visit his personal FaceBook Page at :

https://www.facebook.com/shareef.abdurrasheed1
https://zakirflo.wordpress.com

Abees Ul thani
----

calls to me to return
fadalu, fadalu
welcome, join me
alan wa salan
welcome
come to me
we miss you
we remember you
who came from another
world
yet was right at home
in this ancient Egyptian
village
just outside of iskhanderia
they call Alex
short for Alexandria
perhaps the oldest city
on earth
on the Mediterranean coast
still Abees in many ways
remains ancient yet
contemporary
and you my friend love us
and we love you
and Bill and Hulya too

food for thought = education

dazzling

----

display manifest everyday
look around miracles abound
give thanks, bow down
head on the ground
you were created for worship
one (1) true creator
in the end
when soul taken then
but for the test
the rest is rendered
worthless
now and especially latter
he who made you sustains you
look how he made you
body parts, function,
earth
planet of birth in conjunction
flourish
that which will nourish
but then entered mankind
ungrateful, unsatisfied
set out to destroy, undermine
that which was made to facilitate
enough needs for mankind to
give thanks, take heed
rehearse the verse revealed
so that you may attain life
forever sustained for real

food4thought = education

flake

------
like snow
snow-job you know
such is how politricks go
real snow is to behold
not snow-job why?
dem designed to rob
and lie
they take an oath to serve
good of the people
then dem lie ' n ' steal
this is the real deal
ya'll better wake up
this s#! + got to stop
ya'll put these pigs on top
be it by ballot or not
your dam system a crock
checks and balances...NOT!
but again, they reflect a
mental trend
the people are no different
lying, stealing, gambling,
drugging, drinking, hate others
of a darker hue
just cause dem don't look like
you
this is the true red, WHITE, blue
the leaders are you AmeriKKKa
all one together
ya'll deserve each other
if the people lived by truth
thieves ' n ' liars couldn't rule
not to include the exception
whose vision reflects a different
perception

34

Kimberly Burnham

Find yourself in the pattern. As a 28-year-old photographer, Kimberly Burnham appreciated beauty. Then an ophthalmologist diagnosed her with a genetic eye condition saying, "Consider life, if you become blind." She discovered a healing path with insight, magnificence, and vision. Today, 33 years later, a poet and neurosciences expert with a PhD in Integrative Medicine, Kimberly's life mission is to change the global face of brain health. Using health coaching, Reiki, Matrix Energetics, craniosacral therapy, acupressure, and energy medicine, she supports people in their healing from brain, nervous system, and chronic pain issues. As managing editor of Inner Child Magazine, Kimberly's 2019 project is peace, language, and visionary poetry with her recently published book, *Awakenings: Peace Dictionary, Language and the Mind, a Daily Brain Health Program.*

http://www.NerveWhisperer.Solutions
https://www.linkedin.com/in/kimberlyburnham

YOTP October 2019 Kimberly Burnham Nile River Valley
Africa

Seeking Peace in the Midst

Darfûris seek "tokinnaue"
peace from civil war
as if there can be anything civil about war
or good about natural disasters in Old Nubian
an ancient language displaced
by floods in the Nile Valley
a High Dam erected south of Aswân

Lake Nubia began to flood
anything and everything remaining
gone are Nubian lands in Egypt and Northern Sudan
still people find "tokinnaue" and higher ground
in the Kordofan mountains

Searching for Home

For all who remain
displaced and in search of a home
of plenty and peace

Salam, Shalom, Tokinnaue,
Amani, Paix, Nabáda,
Shanti, Údo, Mër, Mir

Ways to say peace in Africa where
"Asindriza" means peace
or literally beautiful heart in Lugbara
of the West Nile region of Uganda

And "Mal" is peace in Nuer where people pray
"Tạnɛ kɛ mal kä ɛ ciaŋ malä wäwä rɛy Thɔth Thudạn"
let peace and stability continue in South Sudan
and "duany" playfully means "to beckon all by winking"

A Woman's Worth

In this land where people called for peace

by the Arabic word "Aman"

a Dongolawi Sudanese fairytale begins

as the king's daughter tells her father

over and over "ten ēndotonum" (that is from your wife)

she implies a man achieves with his wife's support

the king takes all her property

marries her to a lazy pauper

give up she does not

makes her lazy husband work

successfully they build a castle like the king

who has to admit his daughter is right

Elizabeth E. Castillo

Elizabeth Esguerra Castillo is a multi-awarded and an Internationally-Published Contemporary Author/Poet and a Professional Writer / Creative Writer / Feature Writer / Journalist / Travel Writer from the Philippines. She has 2 published books, "Seasons of Emotions" (UK) and "Inner Reflections of the Muse", (USA). Elizabeth is also a co-author to more than 60 international anthologies in the USA, Canada, UK, Romania, India. She is a Contributing Editor of Inner Child Magazine, USA and an Advisory Board Member of Reflection Magazine, an international literary magazine. She is a member of the American Authors Association (AAA) and PEN International.

Web links:

Facebook Fan Page

https://free.facebook.com/ElizabethEsguerraCastillo

Google Plus

https://plus.google.com/u/0/+ElizabethCastillo

Berbers

Proud raiders they are called,
The Amazigh, courageous fighters
Trampled invaders of their land
The Roman's, Arab, and French.

Descendants of the great Pre-Arab,
Chosen ones, Berber, the "Free People"
The Imazighen in antiquity,
Fought for their religion
Stood up for cultural recognition.

Façade

The overcast sky dawned one day
sprinkling dew drops, misty eyes
Casting the smell of old rose and oak trees
Long after the sudden demise of a down pour.

Chirping birds perched high up the trees
Warm brush of a gust of breeze
The sweet giggles of a baby on your lap
The aroma of love finally within your grasp.

If all these are merely facade or a lucid dream
Why do you hold on to the mem'ries long gone
This Deja Vu leaves one to a state of grace
Longing for one fine day to feel your warm embrace.

Distant revelrie, inviting to the senses
Quenches your thirsty soul
Calms a quivering heart
Past, present, and future happening in the Now.

Pitch Black

Tranquility lingers in the air,

Heartbeat is the only sound

Chiming with the rhythm,

Of restless souls in the dark

Whispers of the mystical veil,

Reverberating over the pitch black abyss.

Joe
Paire

Joe Paire

Joseph L Paire' aka Joe DaVerbal Minddancer . . .
is a quiet man, born in a time where civil liberties
were a walk on thin ice. He's been a victim of his
own shyness often sidelined in his own quest for
love. He became the observer, charting life's path.
Taking note of the why, people do what they do. His
writings oft times strike a cord with the
dormant strings of the reader. His pen the rosined
bow drawn across the mind. He comes full-frontal
or in the subtlest way, always expressing in a way
that stimulate the senses.

www.facebook.com/joe.minddancer

Joe Paire

River Of Men

I won't deny my journey will be fraught with peril
Friends and enemies alike seek out a better plot
it's been days since I last saw Egypt
It hasn't rained in years, so I travel on tears
There seems to be an echo in the land

Life, ebbs and flow like tides in flood season
Women tend their grain so close to the womb
There's a myriad of cultures as I float through
Hippopotami are truly Godlike
While Water buffalo swat at tsetse fly

Sediment and nutrients from blue and white mixers
Where would men be without the fruit of his tears
Four thousand miles of deliverance
this land is harsh on the heels
Date palms and lions, both needed, both need it

The Nile with its twisted miles twisted mouths
No man owns the river, it will leave for months
As mans feed dries up, the riverbed is a dirt road
The river men know this place of broken pieces
The river men are never in denial

No More Sunrise

I breathe in this new sky every morning
It's late December in the east
It's snowing in southern California
I'm heading toward the beach
Climate change or planet shift
I now realize the seriousness
Spring birds don't sing anymore

I breath in the new sky every morning
It's the beginning of June in the east
It's burning up in southern California
I'm shoveling snow three feet deep
Climate change or planet shift
Is it too late to believe those scientists?
There's no pumpkin patch this fall

I breath in this new sky every morning
it's early April in the east
It's a beautiful day in southern California
I'm searching for those rare seeds
Climate change or planet shift
Has all those emissions led to this
I can't find a fruit stand anywhere

I breath in this new sky every morning
It's late September in the east
It's raining in southern California
It's raining as well in the east
Climate change or planet shift
The weather however ceased to exist
The sun doesn't rise anymore

Who Knows Rosemarie?

Shared words led to a feeling so strong
Like the words of a song sung in foreign tongue
Music binds us, words define us
Poems remind us, language is art
Who knows Rosemarie?
Who knows the rosary?
Who so poses those three words?
I love you
I do; when I hear a sonnet
When I read prose
When I read those,
whose work thought provoke
who knows what medium can move you
maybe a religious passage that captured your life
A total strangers' words can give light
Suffice (it) to say, The pens equation to might
Who knows Rosemarie? Or any other entity
That, which can inspire desire inspire peace

hülya
n.
yılmaz

A retired Liberal Arts professor, hülya n. yılmaz [sic] is Co-Chair and Director of Editing Services at Inner Child Press International, and a literary translator. Her poetry has been published in an excess of sixty anthologies of global endeavors. Two of her poems are permanently installed in *TelePoem Booth*, a nation-wide public art exhibition in the U.S. She has shared her work in Kosovo, Canada, Jordan and Tunisia. hülya has been honored with a 2018 WIN Award of British Colombia, Canada. She is presently working on three poetry books and a short-story collection. hülya finds it vital for everyone to understand a deeper sense of self and writes creatively to attain a comprehensive awareness for and development of our humanity.

hülya n. yılmaz, Ph.D.

Writing Web Site
hulyanyilmaz.com

Editing Web Site
hulyasfreelancing.com

not a mere valley

what have your river's waters
not managed to bring along?
195,000 years later emerges the echo
of many a song of praise
while with your arms' tireless sway
The Cradle of Civilization still washes ashore

the longest, most bountiful of the world
with its stunning hues of Blue and White
feeding the center and all around your heart
with no sign of exhaustion dragged on the side
shining onto us a light ever so bright

a breathtaking assembly

i am about to eat the new day's first meal
in Nefertiti's legendary presence
the Pharaohs may object
but my soul
uncorrupted
is ready to commune with all
for all

thinking back to last night
Giza's show of "Sound and Light"
while the Pyramids stood upright
having defied many an earthquake
not having once caved in
to the silky sands underneath
standing majestically erect
suggesting a fatal flaw
in the claim of Modernity
that a work by our frail humanity
stood behind these World Wonders

while a sleep-time ago i half-heartedly listened
to the theatrical staging of perhaps one of a kind
my soul entered the Sphinx and the Pyramids
there, i met my past life again
the final musical piece was most-intoxicating
each move left me in contemplative tears
my entire breath-span passed by
my loved ones, once on Earth
assembled before me one by one

i lost count

the eerie procession
became an all-inclusive projection
invisible untouchable mute
nothing to conceptualize
but to conceive only
as Rumi asserted
in his timeless
voluminous
books of
poetry

then, there remained one

i am one
one is what i am
i am all
all is what i am

i am not becoming

i am

here

now

at a train station . . . in Ramses

not only do we lack the language
but the locals' skills in moving about
we are bound to a train station
in our eager attempt to make it to Alexandria
an unplanned trip of wonder, no doubt

our instructions were to catch the 7:15 train
we made it out of our bed in plenty of time
as the ride to Ramses was to take an hour
here already at 6:22
no service at 7:15 – none whatsoever
8:00AM trains . . . full . . . through 10:00

WC visits, all paid up
(yes, the use of ladies' and gents' restrooms
is attached to a fee)
we now sit in a cafeteria upstairs
having ordered something
we had no intent to eat or drink
as we are not quite awake as of yet
our palates showing no desire for anything
at this early time of the day

no available benches anywhere in sight
4+ hours of wait, quite a plight
sleepy bodies, forcing themselves
to stay upright

so . . .
we are living
amid the regional flair for now
many other passengers seem in a daze
some are asleep in a needy hug
united with the cafe's spreads

Alexandria
is promised to be marvelous

tired, extremely tired
and the trip has not even begun
still, in utmost gratitude
for the pending embrace

Teresa E. Gallion

Teresa E. Gallion

Teresa E. Gallion was born in Shreveport, Louisiana and moved to Illinois at the age of 15. She completed her undergraduate training at the University of Illinois Chicago and received her master's degree in Psychology from Bowling Green State University in Ohio. She retired from New Mexico state government in 2012.

She moved to New Mexico in 1987. While writing sporadically for many years, in 1998 she started reading her work in the local Albuquerque poetry community. She has been a featured reader at local coffee houses, bookstores, art galleries, museums, libraries, Outpost Performance Space, the Route 66 Festival in 2001 and the State of Oklahoma's Poetry Festival in Cheyenne, Oklahoma in 2004. She occasionally hosts an open mic.

Teresa's work is published in numerous Journals and anthologies. She has two CDs: *On the Wings of the Wind* and *Poems from Chasing Light*. She has published three books: *Walking Sacred Ground, Contemplation in the High Desert* and *Chasing Light*.

Chasing Light was a finalist in the 2013 New Mexico/Arizona Book Awards.

The surreal high desert landscape and her personal spiritual journey influence the writing of this Albuquerque poet. When she is not writing, she is committed to hiking the enchanted landscapes of New Mexico. You may preview her work at

http://bit.ly/1aIVPNq or *http://bit.ly/13IMLGh*

Nile River

From ancient times until today,
the Nile flows in harmony
with the cycles of nature:
flooding, growing, harvesting.

The River moves through Burundi,
Egypt, Ethiopia, Kenya, Rwanda,
Sudan, Tanzania, Uganda, and
the Democratic Republic of the Congo.

All make claims to this great river,
partake of the rich reward of water,
fertile soil and life-giving crops.
None own the river but are blessed
to have this gift from nature.

Cool Lyrics

Feet soak in cool lyrics,
river salutes in ripples
headed for its destiny.

Summer's intensity still holds
tight to September.
We engage our last heated

conversation, hold our dried
wounds over the water,
let go and the light embraces us.

Light bodies soar in the forest.
The silence of nature
becomes a heavenly experience.

A New Day

Have you ever gazed at a symbol of hope?
Cast your glance on a tree.
Its majesty carries the joys and sorrows
of many generations, never gives up,
always believes a new day cometh.
That is eternal optimism.

The tree knows it is blessed
in the sunlight's arms and the wind's caress,
looks forward to each morning, embraces
evening to rest and renew itself.

Nourishment flows from the heavenly planes
to the roots. The Creator fills the tree
with abundance. There is always love
stored in its outstretched arms and trunk.
Hug a tree and know what hope is like
no matter the trials and tribulations.

Ashok
K.
Bhargava

Ashok Bhargava is a poet, writer, community activist, public speaker, management consultant and a keen photographer. Based in Vancouver, he has published several collections of his poems: Riding the Tide, Mirror of Dreams, A Kernel of Truth, Skipping Stones, Half Open Door and Lost in the Morning Calm. His poetry has been published in various literary magazines and anthologies.

Ashok is a Poet Laureate and poet ambassador to Japan, Korea and India. He is founder of WIN: Writers International Network Canada. Its main objective is to inspire, encourage, promote and recognize writers of diverse genres, artists and community leaders. He has received many accolades including Nehru Humanitarian Award for his leadership of Writers International Network Canada, Poets without Borders Peace Award for his journeys across the globe to celebrate peace and to create alliances with poets, and Kalidasa Award for creative writings.

A River of Milk and Honey

Waves upon waves
Nile tangoes with sunrays
In rhythmic moves
Of all possible ways

Mother of civilization
Cradle of mankind
Words of a poem
Intellect of a mind

Story of heartthrobs
Love of an outbreak
Pulse of humanity
Never ever fake

Spur of the soil
Germ of all life
Under flames of the sun
Water of rife

What couldn't Last, Lasts

On waking up
I find my body has been rearranged.

My imagination floats
on the waves of time
seeking ships moored at Kochi
and Vasco Da Gama
inhaling southern breeze
laced with black pepper aroma
under a coconut tree.

Carelessly we click photos
of the pale stone the Lisbon monastery
nobody seems to care
who discovered
the sea route to India.

His remains exhumed, moved and
reburied here
to ensure what couldn't last,
lasts.

* Vasco da Gama was a Portuguese explorer and the first European to reach Kochi, India in 1497 by sea from the southern tip of Africa i.e. Cape of Good Hope, which linked Europe and Asia, connecting the Atlantic and the Indian oceans and therefore, the West and the Orient.

I Know But What Do I Know?

Soul is eternal
Imperishable
It comes together
And it comes apart
Can move on from one life to another
Like the rivers run into the sea
But why
I don't know

Read me a sermon
Write it on my lips
With your kisses
Love me
Hold me
Capsize me
Make me sink
dissolve
Vanish

To satiate my knowing
What I do not know

Caroline
'Ceri Naz'
Nazareno

Carolin 'Ceri' Nazareno

Caroline Nazareno-Gabis a.k.a. Ceri Naz, born in Anda, Pangasinan known as a 'poet of peace and friendship', is a multi-awarded poet, journalist, editor, publicist, linguist, educator, and women's advocate.

Graduated cum laude with the degree of Bachelor of Elementary Education, specialized in General Science at Pangasinan State University. Ceri have been a voracious researcher in various arts, science and literature. She volunteered in Richmond Multicultural Concerns Society, TELUS World Science, Vancouver Art Gallery, and Vancouver Aquarium.

She was privileged to be chosen as one of the Directors of Writers Capital International Foundation (WCIF), Member of the Poetry Posse, one of the Board of Directors of Galaktika ATUNIS Magazine based in Albania; the World Poetry Canada and International Director to Philippines; Global Citizen's Initiatives Member, Association for Women's rights in Development (AWID) and Anacbanua. She has been a 4th Placer in World Union of Poets Poetry Prize 2016, Writers International Network-Canada ''Amazing Poet 2015'', The Frang Bardhi Literary Prize 2014 (Albania), the sair-gazeteci or Poet-Journalist Award 2014 (Tuzla, Istanbul, Turkey) and World Poetry Empowered Poet 2013 (Vancouver, Canada).

Shamata

i can hear you,
from the celestial sphere of souls,
so i listen to my body, my mind and my heart,
drowning in placid horizons,
i can see you,
from the light particles,
spectrum and radiance
of neutron stars,
connecting all the sacred spaces
between our destiny;
i become the sound
in the echoing, unheard lullabies,
i become the silence
from the soothing miracles
of the unruffled time.

Ubuntu

"I am because we are,"
"humanity towards others

We are travellers,
in the interconnectedness
of our DNA, tied to be whole
together.
We are creators,
of justice; so we uplift equality,
no one is left behind,
the open-heartedness of a blessed
shares the humanity's spell,
We are held to sacrifice
For one another
Because I am you,
You are me,
Yes, we are one.

Growing with you

Let us grow together
Under the sun
Under the rain,
Whenever there is growth,
That yields from our hearts,
We become sweet, better fruits.
Let us grow joy,
As we feel pain and sorrow
For tomorrow's another day
To live and be loved.
Let us grow and bloom
As the rainbow speaks hope
And the rays of the sun
Brings forth life,
And when I grow with you,
We can do well,
Embracing the sun and the rain.

Swapna Behera

Swapna Behera is a bilingual contemporary poet, author, translator and editor from Odisha, India .She was a teacher from 1984 to 2015 . Her stories, poems and articles are widely published in National and International journals, and ezines, and are translated into different national and International languages. She has penned four books. She was conferred upon the Prestigious International Poesis Award of Honor at the 2nd Bharat Award for Literature as Jury in 2015, The Enchanting Muse Award in India World Poetree Festival 2017, World Icon of Peace Award in 2017, and the Pentasi B World Fellow Poet in 2017.. She is the recipient of Gold Cross Of Wisdom Award ,the medal for The Best Teachers of the World from World Union of Poets in 2018, and The LIfe time Achievement Award ,The Best Planner Award, The Sahitya Shiromani Award, ATAL BiHARI BAJPAYEE AWARD 2018, Ambassador De Literature Award 2018 .She is the Ambassador of Humanity by Hafrikan Prince Art World Africa 2018 and an official member of World Nation's Writers Union ,Kazakhstan2018. At present she is the manager at Large, Planner and Columnist of The Literati, the administrator of several poetic groups ,the member of the Special Council of Five of World Union of Poets and the Cultural Ambassador of Inner Child Press U.S.

Innocence On The Palette

the calendar delivers
the paramount truth
few steps to the silent valley
speaks, twits, cries, shouts
may be; it celebrates ....

golden paddy stems
or the pigeons on the temple
extended hands of the school kids during the short break
the Sun rays on the grave yard or in the courtyard of a sex
worker
innocence thou art the virgin eyes
a vision or a mission
million of tear drops together or a crescent smile
mirror of the galaxy
some moments
river in the ocean
a diagram or a diaphragm
each innocent soul fixes multiple
do or die agendas
yes, innocence is the rainbow on the

palette

In Conversation With The Nile ....

she is the life line
 that flows
from south to north

 the mother of men and father of life
the milky way is the celestial mirror
of her lusty loops
 mystical harper in the dawn
 sitting on the Aswan dam
plays duets with the nimbus
the cotton farmer rushing to the field
the Nile carries dark silt
as a pregnant woman

it speaks and writes the history of civilisation
and geography of pollutions
"how long shall I carry the cyanotoxins?
allow me to reach the Mediterranean
 my destination"

valley that grows wheat, barley and papyrus
the White Nile
the Blue Nile and
the Atbara from Ethiopia
all three tributaries join.
to sing a common melody
 the eternal song....

can you listen the splash and murmuring?
 river is certainly a
constitution; a responsibility
of yours and mine ....

come with me !

come with me
I will show you the tattoo
on the face of the globe
the melting iceberg
 fear of Greta Thunberg

Come with me
we will stop a while
the nature cries
tears have become fears

come with me
leave your lap top for awhile
we will plant trees
 create a forest
with seed balls

come with me
 we will again build
 and generate
someone has to start somewhere
then why not you or me?

come with me
let us clean
before the dawn ....

Albert 'Infinite' Carrasco

I'm a project life philanthropist, I speak about the non ethical treatment of poor ghetto people. Why? My family was their equal, my great grandmother and great grandfather was poor, my grandmother and grandfather, my mother and father, poverty to my family was a sequel, a traditional Inheritance of the subliminal. I paid attention to the decades of regression, i tried to make change, but when I came to the fork in the road and looked at the signs that read wrong < > right, I chose the left, the wrong direction, because of street life interactions a lot around me met death or incarceration. I failed myself and others. I regret my decisions, I can't reincarnate dead men, but I can give written visions in laymens. I'm back at that fork in the road, instead of it saying wrong or right, I changed it, now it says dead men < > life.

Infinite poetry @lulu.com

Alcarrasco2 on YouTube

Infinite the poet on reverbnation

Infinite Poetry

http://www.lulu.com/us/en/shop/al-infinite-carrasco/infinite-poetry/paperback/product-21040240.html

North Africa

Arabs, Berbers, Arab berbers, Tuareg people and Bedouin
make up this region.
Tunisia, Egypt, Morocco, Sudan, Algeria, West sahara,
Mauritania and Libya are countries in this area.
There's so much to see from Cairo to Tripoli,
Like the great Sphinx,
museums holding king Tut artifacts and royal mummies.
Here the Nile river flows,
Mauresque architecture shows
Moorish and European art Deco.
It's home of of a centuries old Medina and the Bardo.
Islam and Christianity are the main religions,
Arabic is the dialect mostly spoken.

A dark place

I'm from a dark place where, I'm struggling, I'm depressed, my back is against the wall and I need a shoulder to lean on is written on everyday peoples face. Where I'm from It can be summer, bright outside and hot like a oven, but the sun doesn't shine often. Poverty had parents shopping on credit at the corner store, they weren't lazy people they just needed the opportunity to work, save money and build up credit scores. Hustlers are made where I'm from, settling for less wasn't everyone's decision. I've seen people work on engines and transmissions on main streets. I know people that'll fix your washing machine and dryer for a few dollars. I know an old man that walked the hood looking for old or broken shopping carts, he'll use four to make one then sell it, walking the hood yelling "last call, I wouldn't wait one minute". When there's will there's a way, us children of circumstance running the streets in search of fun will become the ones who run the streets in search of funds with guns and hard ya. We was in a dark place living at a fast pace, we'd rather ride in the back of hearses instead of living under traditional curses. That's exactly what happened, a lot of men lost vitals trying to break the cycle. Hustling was opportunity to my generation, we went hard for dead prez accumulation, when you do accumulate money, it instantly becomes an addiction. I was addicted and so was my homies, we didn't want rehab, we were cash junkies, we o.d'd daily trying to get high enough to never go back to poverty.

Knowledge is to know

We walked through the flames on the surface of hell to put food on our plates, coke and dope was on the menu, the streets was how we ate, RIP to the fallen, when it's my turn meet me at the pearly gates. I went to funerals and saw eyes and lips glued up, kissed foreheads, mourned the dead, then went right back to the trap to get rid of my last re-up. Unfortunately death wasn't a deterrent, it came along with the risk and wish of moving out of housing developments. If I say losing day ones didn't hurt I'll be lying, it hurts bad, I'll be in my bag poppn at anyone for anything, tears didn't drop, slugs flying and shells falling was me crying.

I'll do anything to walk side by side home base victims of homicide again, it'll be incredible to look to the left and right and see a lot of old friends. Since that's not possible I'll keep walking this blood thirsty sphere with those still here. It's a smaller circle with the same goals, but with different opportunities, we're hustln hard and grindn daily without lean and nose candy. Harsh lessons were taught, painful knowledge was gained, we wanted to reign, it rained, it was a blood flood.

Eliza Segiet

Eliza Segioet

After earning a Master's Degree in Philosophy at the Jagiellonian University in Krakaw, Poland, Eliza Segiet proceeded with her post-graduate studies in the fields of Cultural Knowledge, Penal Revenue and Economic Criminal Law, Arts and Literature and Film and Television Production in the Polish city, Lodz.

With specific regard to her creative writings, the author describes herself as being torn in her passion for engaging in two literary genres: Poetry and Drama. A similar dichotomy from within is reflected on Segiet's own words about her true nature: She likes to look at the clouds, but she keeps both of her feet set firmly on the ground.

The author describes her worldview as being in harmony with that of Arthur Schopenhauer: "Ordinary people merely think how they shall 'spend' their time; a man of talent tries to 'use' it".

Abyss of Oblivion

They still look
for the treasures of the past
to
touch
– understand
the enormity of the human
thought and work.

In the dark kingdom,
for a return towards the light
await
the silently slain acts.

To extract from the abyss of oblivion,
to give a new life
– to restore the memory.

Among the Saharan sands,
a long-lost civilization
does not allow itself to be
forgotten.

The world
needs testimonies
to
draw near the hidden secrets.

translated by Artur Komoter

Accoucheurs

Accoucheurs of the past

reveal the past moments,

so in the murmur of the walls

to be able to see yesterday.

translated by Artur Komoter

Mirage

I was a grain of sand in the desert,
a droplet of the ocean,
a flame coming out
of a glowing hot fire,
the wind delicately lashing
worn out hands.

In the sun-warmed desert
I transformed into
a dune, the ocean, heat, a gale.
I am the fickleness, a chameleon, the element.
I am the volcano.

I feel the ardour under my feet,
and in the distance I see you
running towards my thirsty lips.
I've waited so long!

You are now just for me,
I have you at my fingertips.

Why are you running for so long?
Why are you disappearing?
I cannot believe!
You were a mirage!

translated by Artur Komoter

William
S.
Peters Sr.

Bill's writing career spans a period of over 50 years. Being first Published in 1972, Bill has since went on to Author in excess of 40 additional Volumes of Poetry, Short Stories, etc., expressing his thoughts on matters of the Heart, Spirit, Consciousness and Humanity. His primary focus is that of Love, Peace and Understanding!

Bill says . . .

I have always likened Life to that of a Garden. So, for me, Life is simply about the Seeds we Sow and Nourish. All things we "Think and Do", will "Be" Cause and eventually manifest itself to being an "Effect" within our own personal "Existences" and "Experiences" . . . whether it be Fruit, Flowers, Weeds or Barren Landscapes! Bill highly regards the Fruits of his Labor and wishes that everyone would thus go on to plant "Lovely" Seeds on "Good Ground" in their own Gardens of Life!

to connect with Bill, he is all things Inner Child

www.iaminnerchild.com

Personal Web Site

www.iamjustbill.com

Nile

From the bowels of creation
Ushered forth was a land
That is known
Which wields
Mankind's Fertile Crescent

In the lands
Is the womb
that gave birth
To civilization
And civility
To untold nations
Who to this day
Claim it
As their own convention
Along with the invention
Of history . . .
His-Story

But Mother has a story of Her own!

Listen !!!!

So I did

She sharpened the pencil . . . deliberately
Then raised it on high
Above her spiritual aura
And then stabbed me . . .
Again deliberately
In my heart

She began to etch
Words and verse,
Lyrics dispersed
Upon the walls
Of my cluttered chambers of love . . .
In a 'Free-Style" sort of way,
For that is how her spirit was . . . FREE

We had no use for the eraser
During this life defying,
Edifying moment,
So, we took it, together
Between our fingers
And began to eliminate, erase
All the dimly lit vibrations about us
That expectorated anything less
Than brilliance

And then the music played,
Once again
As it had done
O so long ago
In the days of my youth

I thanked her
For the gift,
This perceivable world,
Where I let and bled

All the poisons
I have ingested
And collected
Along my selected, defected . . . way

I smiled as I reflected
And inspected
The 'who am I',
And I remembered succinctly
That I loved to dance . . .
So I did

Out there huh?

Push button memories
And
Instant daisies
Growing out of that pot I sketched
In my note book
While sitting on
My Blue Roof
In my Blue Moment

Kent Newburn says to me
That these times
Are keepers,
Jeepers mom,
Can you play that back
Again?

Kent Newburn says to me
That these times
Are keepers

We too often forget
What is important ...
Is it the memories
We create and construct
In our dimly lit halls
Of cognizance?
Or the flowers we produce
Along the way ...
Chances are,
It's a hodge podge

Say,
What was Alice's boyfriend's name,
Did he go to Wonderland as well,
If so, I betcha by golly wow,

She will never tell ...

In the meantime
All the Kings and Princes
And a few Princesses too,
The Governors and Rulers,
And Oligarchs few
Sang in concert
The Lechers Anthem
While on the hunt
For innocence
To be defiled ...
Keep a very close eye
On your child and children,
For they are not safe
In this world
That has been heralded ...
In and out
The revolving door goes
While we are far too busy
Sticking our noses
Where it does not belong,
Like up the wrong asses

The other day
While sitting in class
At Film School
I wrote a script,
Kind of silly of sort
About how we can abort
All of the nonsense
Before we all
Are poisoned ....

I really did not want to share
Such an ominous thing,
So I wrote this poem instead

About all the crazy stuff
Floating around
In my head ...

The only thing is,
I can not remember
Whether or not
This is a push button memory
Or something I sketched
Called 'Instant Daisies' ...
Out there huh?

William S. Peters, Sr.

October
2019
Featured Poets

~ * ~

Ngozi Olivia Osuoha

Denisa Kondić

Pankhuri Sinha

Christena AV Williams

i FLY

because I Can

... said the Dreamer to the world.

www.iamjustbill.com

Ngozi
Olivia
Osuoha

NGOZI OLIVIA OSUOHA is a Nigerian poet / writer / thinker. A graduate of Estate Management with experience in Banking and Broadcasting. She has published over one hundred poems / articles in over ten countries. Her first two longest poems of 355 and 560 verses titled THE TRANSFORMATION TRAIN and LETTER TO MY UNBORN published in Kenya and Canada respectively are available on Amazon. She has also featured in over ten international anthologies/books/blogs. She is a passionate African ink.

Storms

Of the waves that sink
And the waters we drink,
None is the food we eat
Rather, the flood that did defeat.

Of the earthquakes that destroy
And the landslides that toy,
None can our joy deploy
Because there is no peace to employ.

Of the winds that blow
And the storms that grow,
None can our love flow
For they bring us so low.

Storms so strange
Local and foreign, at range
Storms that change
Stories, histories, eternal.

Lingering Effect

If we write the storm
It comes like worm,
If we paint the picture
It dribbles our nature,
If we make a collage
We study it at college,
A perfect lingering effect.

We do not want to die
Hence, the knot we tie
We love to live
So we cherish what we give,
We defeat the battle
Even without our cattle,
For we must move on.

The path of tide
And the length of time
The part so wide
And the strength against crime
There, we pitch our tent
For life is so bent
Even as we pay rent.

Flames

Raged and angered ocean
Thundering and thunderous sea,
Noisy wind and restless breeze
Troubled land and besieged souls,
Only God understands.

Weeping voices and wailing victims
Floating houses and sinking homes,
Hopeless people and dying nation
Only God knows.

Animals and beasts that raze
Humans and beings at gaze
Souls and spirits ablaze,
A world in flames
Losing her games
Evil gaining names.

Not Withstanding

The Caribbean tears
Mingling down the Nile,
The European gears
Going extra mile
The African fears
Haunting the file
The Asian wears
Flowing the tile,
The American years
Curing pile,
The Australian bears
Not looking fragile.

A lingering effect
Disasters, natural and devastating
Yet never frightening her
As she hopes life never ends
Loving life to wait for hope
Living it lively to the fullest,
The Caribbean hope
Across that tiny rope
Reaching heights and highs
Nervous with sighs,
The hurricanes not withstanding.

Denisa Kondić

Denisa Kondić

Denisa Kondić is a published poet, reviewer and a translator, as well as a humanist and an advocate for the rights of children.

She is also widely published in collections with other authors and has participated in many international poetry festivals.

Crumpled Bridge

On a stream that follows me all my life,
I choke tears in my bosom.
I do not let them fall into a gray turmoil
That is turbid from others' iron scraps.
They are salty and keep memories from oblivion,
Conserving me from pain and disintegration.

This is my river,
Where did it go?
This is my road,
Why did you crash it down?
Spite seethes in her tendons -
target.
On people faces I don't see plain ground
Its furrows are turned into wrinkles,
Scowls are engraved in their hearts
Spite is on their palms -
target.

But my road, my beloved bridge,
Like a crumpled A3 format,
Larger than other formats,
Gapes.

Had it only been a behemoth
Showing its jaws after a fair strife,
Leaving its skeleton in the waters.
If only it is not -
target.

I look, with a frost-bound spirit,
I become an apparition, not to stick out.
At least, I've got a place,
I will make it to the other bank
Before the dark, before the sirens,

And its deadly wail,
Cries.

My mother is waiting,
I have to see her,
All the memories of a crumpled paper
I have to leave behind.
On that iron paper,
I write in thoughts:
"You were a giant to me
Every time I crossed you
On a bike, or barefoot,
Or when I flew over you in dreams.
Now you are a corpse stretched out"
target.

Had this April 1st
Only been a prank
Rage will arise in me
I would protect myself.
But now, unprepared for the reality
I bow down my head, choking tears.
But you did not defeat me,
I am from the Balkans.

A last glance on Petrovaradin
From the other bank
I don't let a tear fall
I have to save a remembrance
for my future self.

Target: During the NATO bombing of Serbia, after several bridges were destroyed by bombs, people decided to protect the rest of the bridges with their bodies. In great numbers, they would wear shirts that had the word "Target" and a bullseye graphic and would stand on the bridges during signs of air attack, hoping to prevent damage to the bridge.

"I don't have a name"

I was born just before the bombs
In a village in Kosovo.
Invisible before society
Unimportant for the world.

They didn't register me
The bombs prevented them.
Where a name should stand
"No name" is written.

Hey, you big world,
Hear me, I am existing
I do not have a name
But I have myself.

I grew up on mother's milk
It is the same for all the kids
But I am double cursed:
Being from Kosovo and dark skinned.

Years are counted the same for all
Being Gypsies or others
But we steal happiness differently
And hide it just to be shown.

But I am twenty this year
I mock the injustice and don't care
But the the bombs remind me
That a name I don't have.

*(A true story of a Gypsy girl who didn't have an official
name in her personal papers until this year)*

Beneath The End

This shelter is atramentous
a remembrance on the soul crawls
I am banished, harshly stepped on
On the skin your words sharply scrawl.

Throw a mask, dare to be a man
It is better seen when it's dark
You gave a word when it was light
But now shots are the only marks.

Aimed with soft words of eloquence
As a statue you're standing there
Promises that you ran over
Be courageous to count. Be here!

Come and rest now on my warm lap
My soul is wide as a flat land
My arms are long, soft, firm and bare
Of explosions I am not scared.

I escaped death in a moment
Carved a new image of myself.
But because of dread you became
A pillar of salt, shame - thyself.

In this cold aphonic shelter
I shattered tears of my lone soul
Got the shot into my bosom
And buried you, for good, in whole.

Denisa Kondić

Pankhuri Sinha

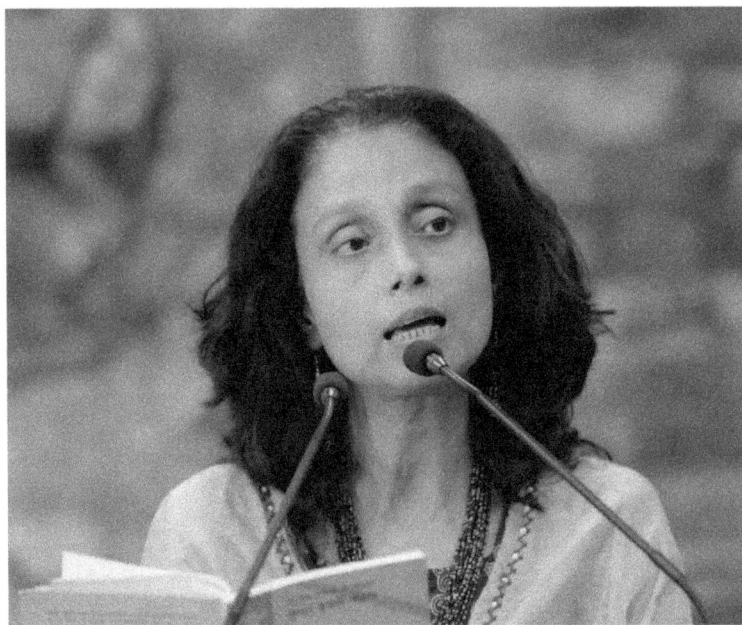

Pankhuri Sinha is an bilingual young poet and story writer, just starting my first novel. Have two books of Poems Published in English- Dear Suzannah, and Prison Talkies. Have two collections of stories published in Hindi, and four collections of poetries published in Hindi, and many more of both are lined up. Have won several prestigious, national awards for my writings in Hindi. Currently, teach History and Hindi Literature in a graduate college in India. Have an incomplete Phd, in History from the University of Calgary, Alberta, Canada, and an MA in History from SUNY Buffalo. Date of Birth 18th June, 1975. As a woman, I write for gender equality among many things.

After the rabbits had changed their colors

Before the snow,
They planned
A hunting trip
Some place, nearby
They got some guns
Real guns
Knowing all were not friends
But they united
It seems, over guns
And sailed off.
But these lines are for those
Who knew of hunting
And stayed back
Watching the rabbits change their colors.

Closing Before Time

The cafes
Closing, just as I get there
Not even, as they see me come
But right before that
So sound is the surveillance network
Thus
Performing the final act of closing
Exactly as I reach
And to say
Very politely with a smile
Sorry
We are closed

In the days, when you are
Living By the Taste of Your Drink
Among a lot of bitterness
Of unnecessary conflicts….

You Know
We all do know of it
The endless war over nothing
Just embittering all things sweet
Including the coco and vanilla
In my tall
Americano Coffee
The two things I like to sprinkle
Or load it with
By coolly walking by
Just as I pour complementary cream
And worse
Begin opening plain sugar saches's in one's drink
Doing it time after time…….

The Place of One's Drink in Total Friendlessness

The Place of One's Drink in Total Friendlessness
Is a thing we all must understand
You cannot drink very sweet drinks
In very bitter days
Or can you?
Should I take the recommendation of the stranger.....

These are not days of slavery
On the sugar plantations
But as the Arab Spring
Beginning In Tunisia
Told us
Things are not pleasant
On Fruit plantations
Either in the Caribbean, or in dear old India
Or Africa
And no
This poem is not about Ebola
Outbreak or treatment
In the once German colonies
Of the Congos

And I am not boycotting sugar
Just that my grandmum could not
Get her hip operated upon
Because of alarming levels of blood sugar

Doesn't mean I am eager
For a hip, or a knee or an intestinal operation
I fear the latter the most
For they have ruined it completely

I am doing coke, ice cream
Tea and coffee for food
Well, mostly

More than my stomach
My heart is a wreck
And the trouble is
There is no remedy in sight

I have never lived in such friendlessness
Not even friendlessness
Neither a Vacuum
An emptiness
But a constant assertion
By all
That they are not friends
That they will not be friends
Till I do
As they say
And
Most certainly
My walking into starbucks
Getting the soy lattes
And extra chocolate Mocha
Is problematic.

Pankhuri Sinha

Christena
AV
Williams

Christena AV Williams

Christena AV Williams is a Jamaican multiple award-winning Author and an ICPI Cultural ambassador. She Holds a BA (Hons.) In History (major) and Philosophy (minor) from The University of the West Indies. Her Book, "Pearls among Stones" was awarded Prime Ministers National Youth Awards for excellence in Arts and Culture.

Some of her featured works are: Gleaner newspaper, Poetry NZ 47 in New Zealand, Tuck magazine, shortlisted in Desmond O' Grady poetry in Ireland, featured Poet at Jamaica Poetry festival, and An assistant instructor to Poet laureate, Lorna Goodison in All flowers are roses programme and youth4peaceJA ambassador.

Black Magic

Good morning jaw-dropping melanin Kings and Queens
Have the sun kissed your cheeks?
Have the wind greet you with a surreal embrace?
Did the bees hum your name?
Did the birds chirp the peace you exudes?
Did the ants fall in rows kneeling at your feet
Awaiting your command?
Did the trees bow at such Black magical Beings?
Can you contain such an energy field?
Does nature show its reverence when you exhale?
Did you hear the angels singing your praises?
Did you thank your creator for making you and me?
So, Good Morning your majesty.

Heart Transplant

Crashing paper planes on the beating drums
Still life,
Resuscitate a poor, poor heart that malfunctions
As I am too weak to whisper, "save me"
Too cold to forgive my prisoner as I am locked in
Guantanamo bay.

Too broken to find a new heart
Too sick to care if I live or die
Strung up on tubes walking around
Loveless
Spaced out, head bound on a
Never ending carousal
While you stroll nirvana
Alluring souls
Painless.

This heart deteriorates by the seconds
Hallucinating on fading memories
Which fumes intoxication in my lungs,
Liver and heart
Now I am on life support.

I am up all nights towards the morning
Coughing up shock waves
Puking butterflies

In bed I lay awake from the nightmares
Of elm street of us
At times the sunrise escapes my windows
Which reminds me of a cherished portrait of you
I wished to deny its nocturnal majesty
But I long the eternal.

In the tropics

It is a restless sea
There is no place I rather be
Than in your arms, harmoniously
Been thinking for a while
That we need to get away
From the bigotry into paradise.

The waves whisper our names
The sun intensifies our soul
We scream and exhale
Our banana leaf flesh symmetrically sprawled out
In the cabana
As the coconut trees dance to our beating hearts.

The aroma of roasted yams and breadfruit
And cooked ackee and saltifsh
Whet our appetites
Could we ask for more?
This place is mystic to the eyes
Our spirit is one with the ancestors
We are at home.

Baby can we relax into each other's
Eyes and beam at the stars
While we swing in the hammock
And you caress my hips to thighs
Bite my lips
Kiss my feet to butt cheeks
Slowly reaching up to my nose
To my forehead
And back again to lips
To the tree arches in my paradise
Can we be whisked away in the tropics?

Remembering

our fallen soldiers of verse

Janet Perkins Caldwell

February 14, 1959 ~ September 20, 2016

Alan W. Jankowski

16 March 1961 ~ 10 March 2017

Inner Child Press

News

Poetry Posse Members

We are so excited to share and announce a few of the current books, as well as the new and upcoming books of some of our Poetry Posse authors.

On the following pages we present to you ...

Jackie Davis Allen

Gail Weston Shazor

hülya n. yılmaz

Nizar Sartawi

Faleeha Hassan

Fahredin Shehu

Caroline 'Ceri' Nazareno

Eliza Segiet

William S. Peters, Sr.

Now Available at

www.innerchildpress.com

No Illusions

Through the Looking Glass

Jackie Davis Allen

Now Available at

www.innerchildpress.com

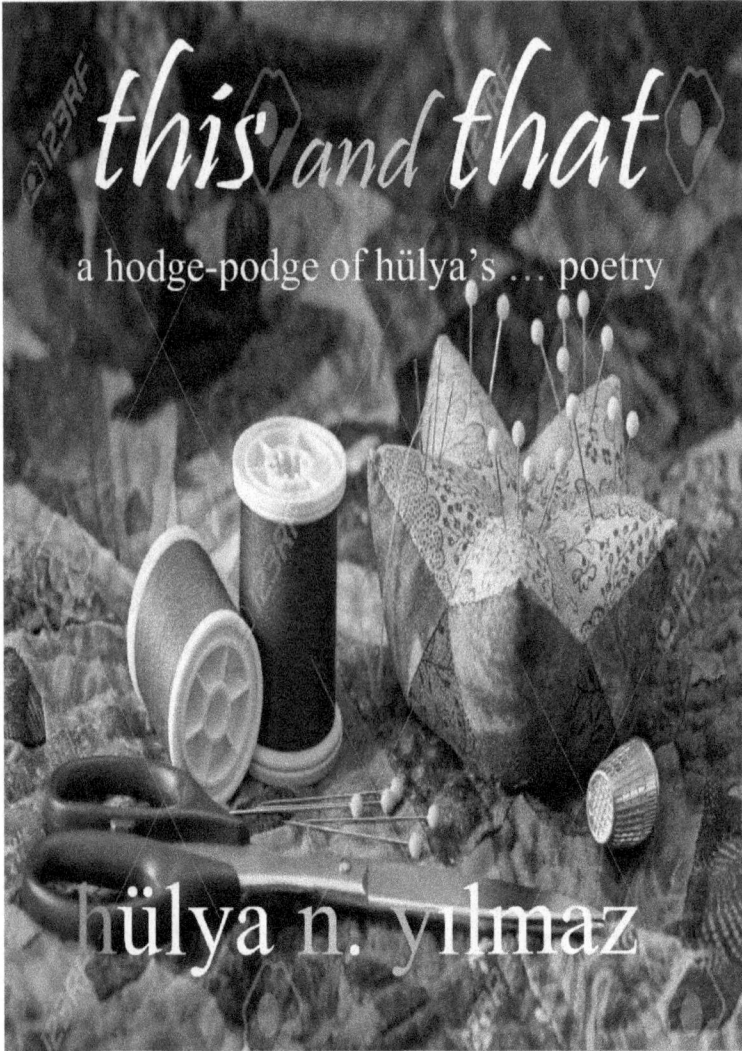

this and that

a hodge-podge of hülya's ... poetry

hülya n. yılmaz

Now Available at

www.innerchildpress.com

Now Available at
www.innerchildpress.com

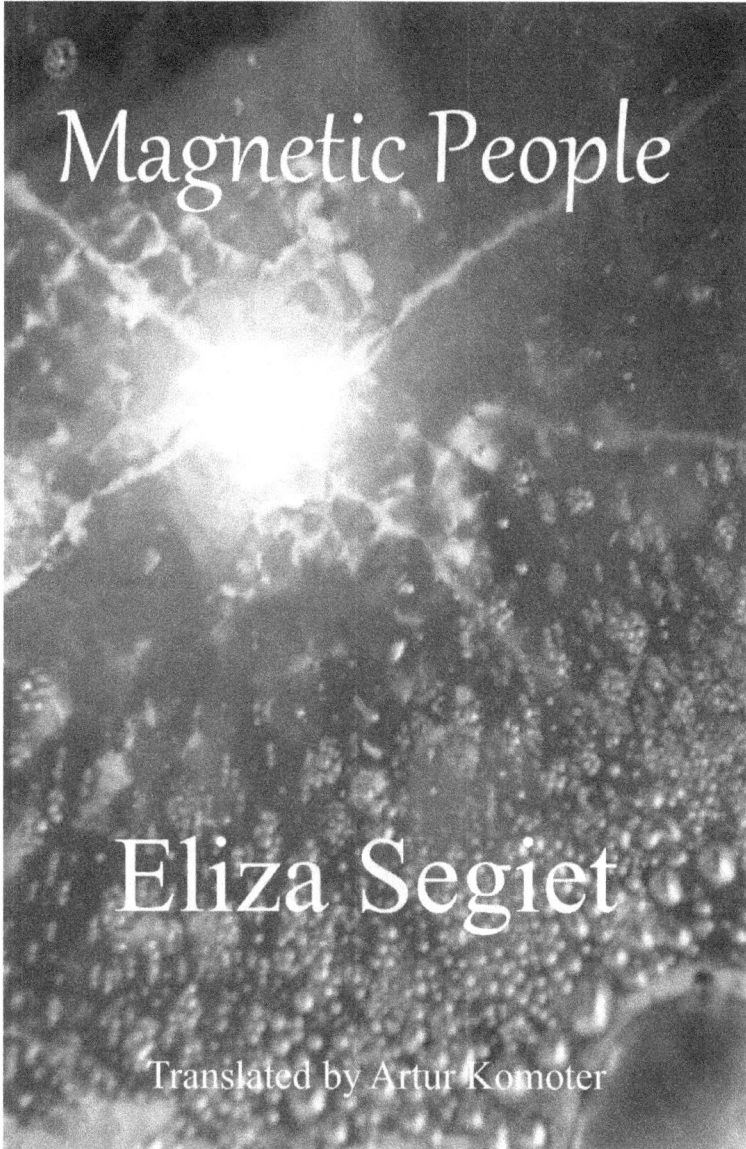

Now Available at
www.innerchildpress.com

Now Available at

www.innerchildpress.com

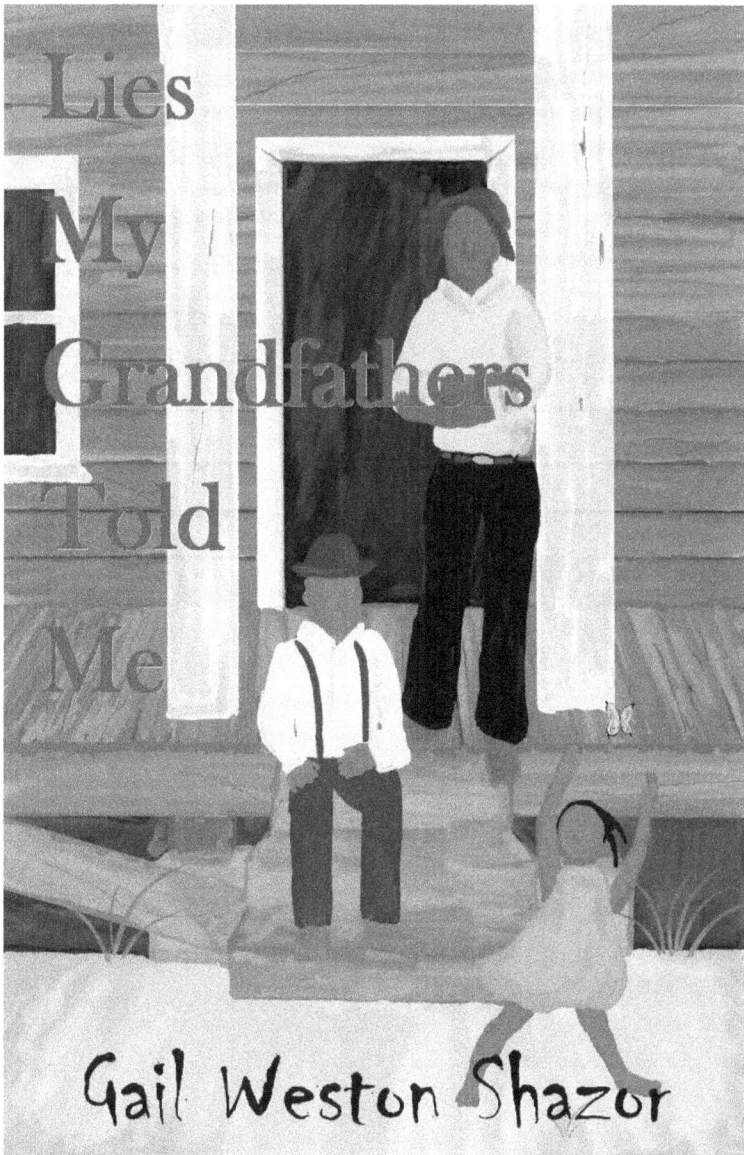

Lies My Grandfathers Told Me

Gail Weston Shazor

Inner Child Press News

Now Available at
www.innerchildpress.com

Aflame

Memoirs in Verse

hülya n. yılmaz

Now Available at
www.innerchildpress.com

Nizar Sartawi

Inner Child Press News

Now Available at
www.innerchildpress.com

Mass Graves

Faleeha Hassan

Now Available at
www.innerchildpress.com

Breakfast

for

Butterflies

Faleeha Hassan

Now Available at
www.innerchildpress.com

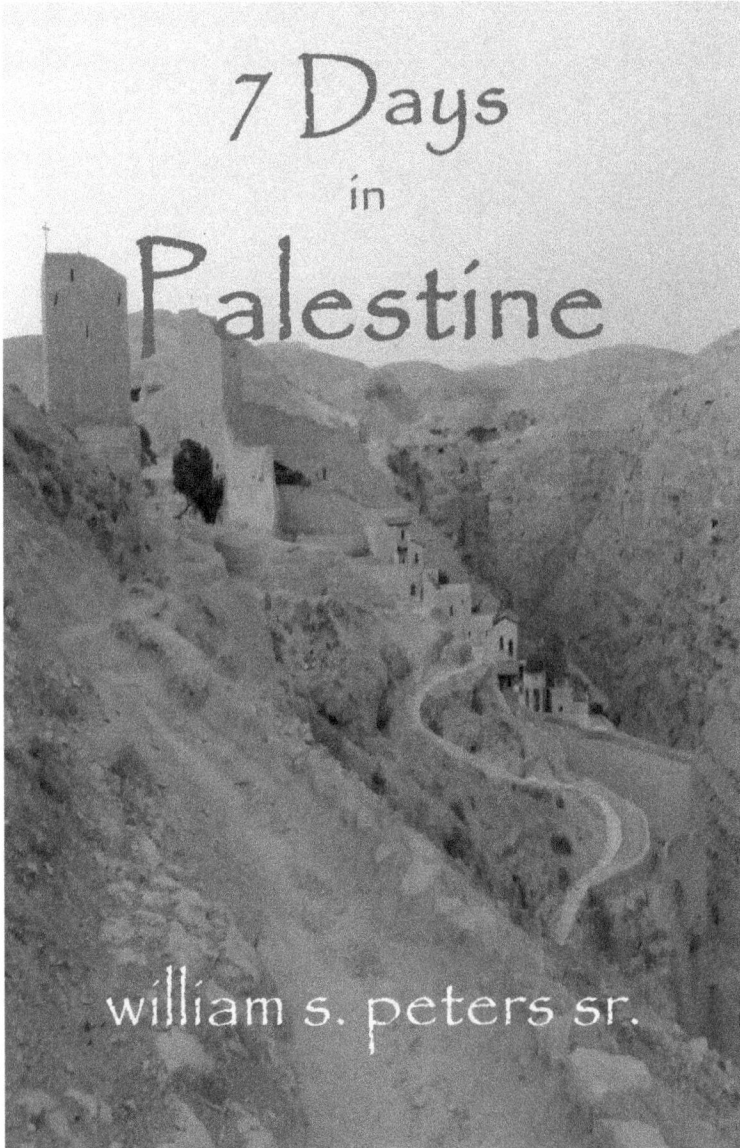

7 Days
in
Palestine

william s. peters sr.

Now Available at
<u>www.innerchildpress.com</u>

inner child press
presents

Tunisia My Love

william s. peters, sr.

Coming in the Summer of 2019

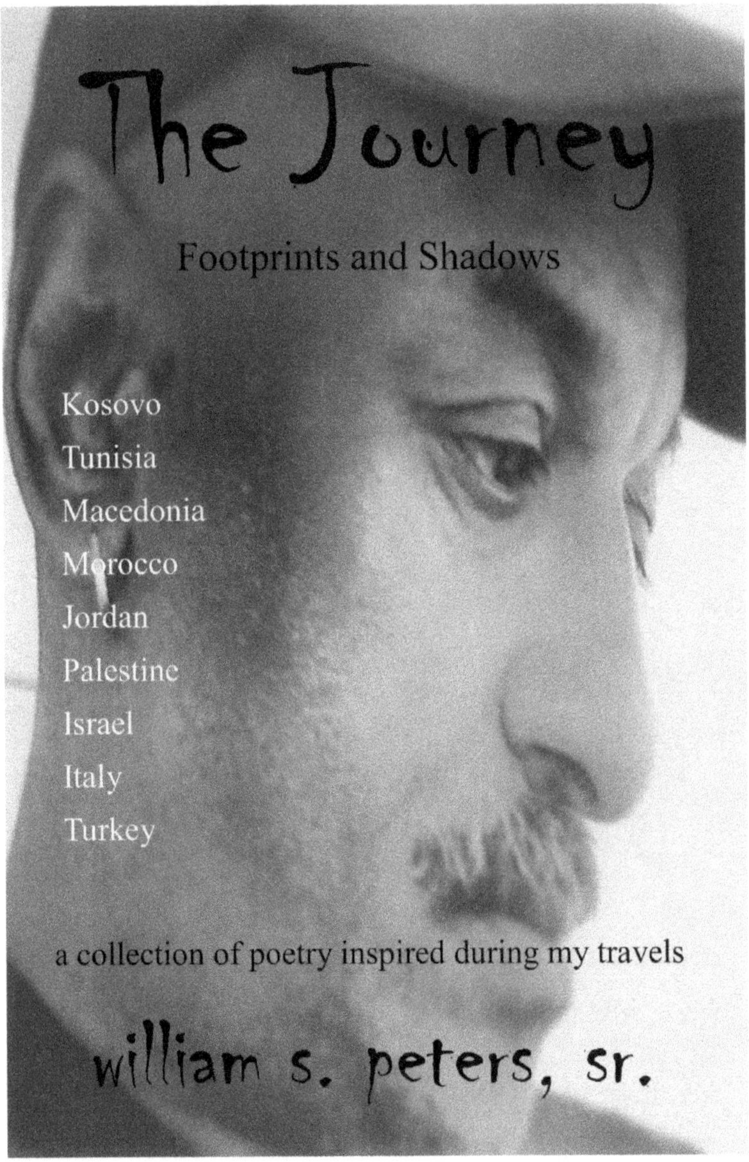

The Journey

Footprints and Shadows

Kosovo
Tunisia
Macedonia
Morocco
Jordan
Palestine
Israel
Italy
Turkey

a collection of poetry inspired during my travels

william s. peters, sr.

Now Available at

www.innerchildpress.com

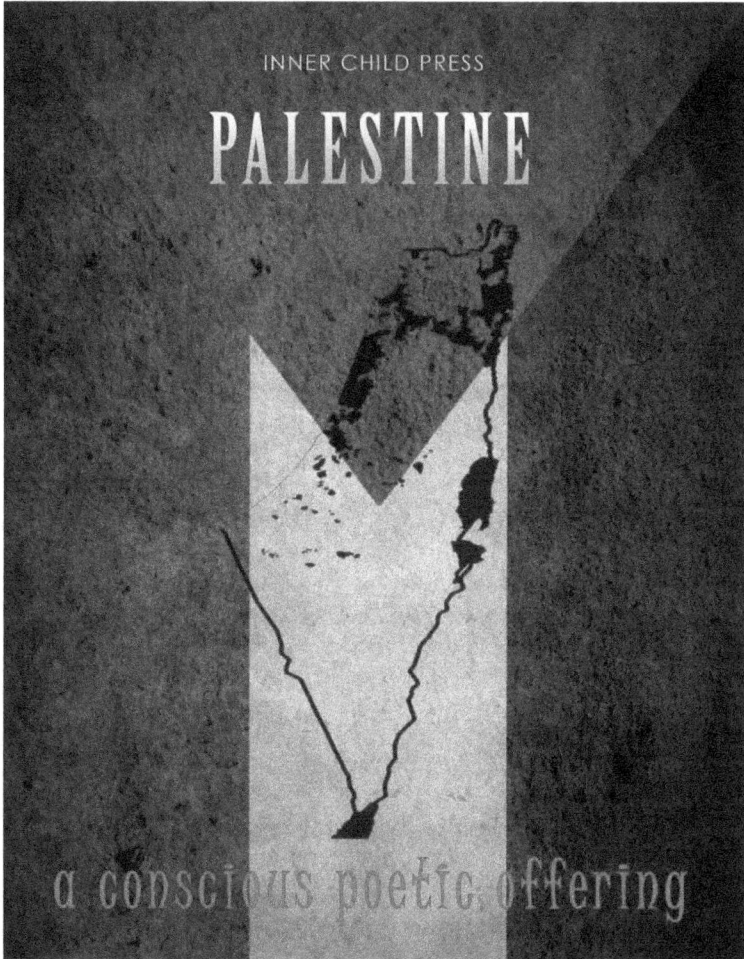

Now Available at
www.innerchildpress.com

Now Available at
www.innerchildpress.com

Now Available at
www.innerchildpress.com

Think on These Things
Book II

william s. peters, sr.

Now Available at
www.innerchildpress.com

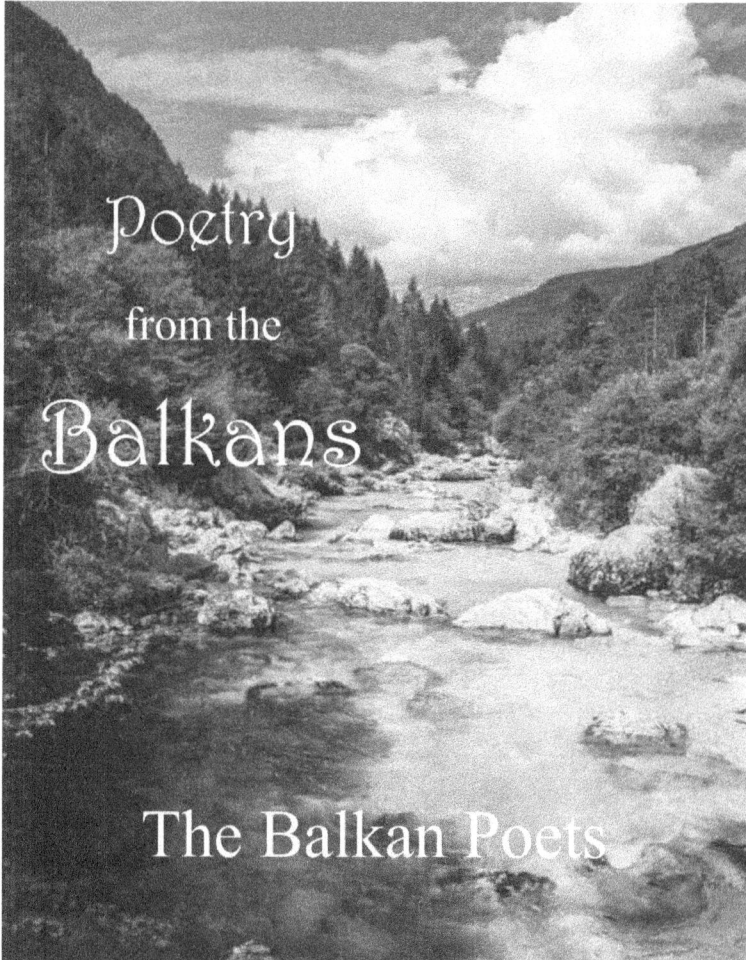

Other

Anthological

works from

Inner Child Press International

www.innerchildpress.com

Inner Child Press International
presents

𝔄 𝔏𝔬𝔳𝔢 𝔄𝔫𝔱𝔥𝔬𝔩𝔬𝔤𝔶
2019

The Love Poets

Now Available

www.worldhealingworldpeacepoetry.com

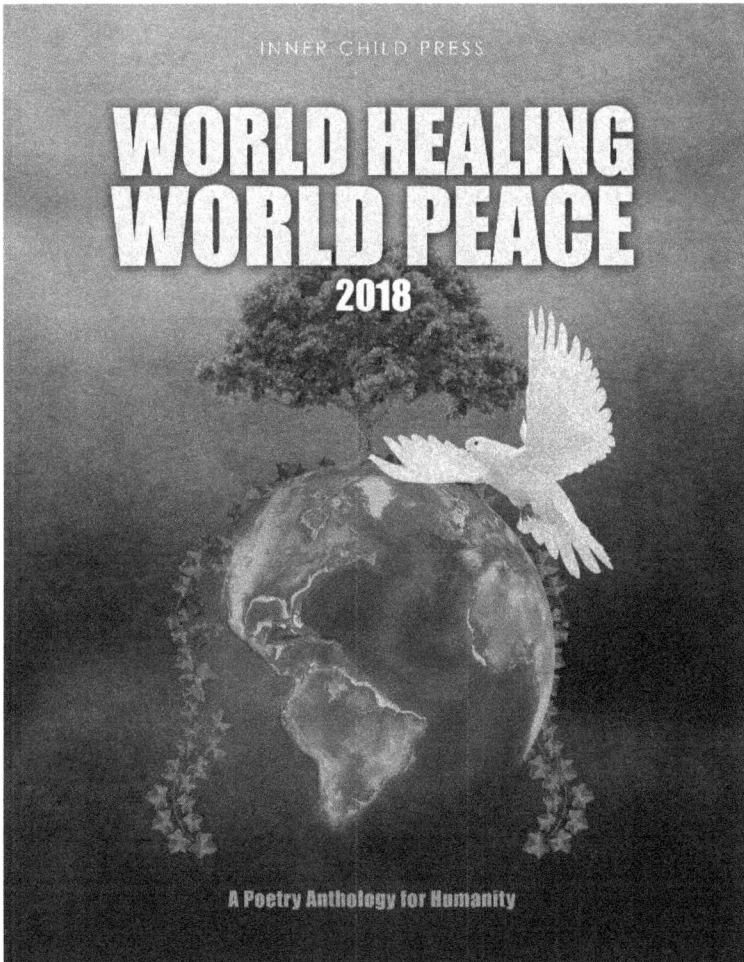

A Poetry Anthology for Humanity

Now Available

www.worldhealingworldpeacepoetry.com

Now Available

www.worldhealingworldpeacepoetry.com

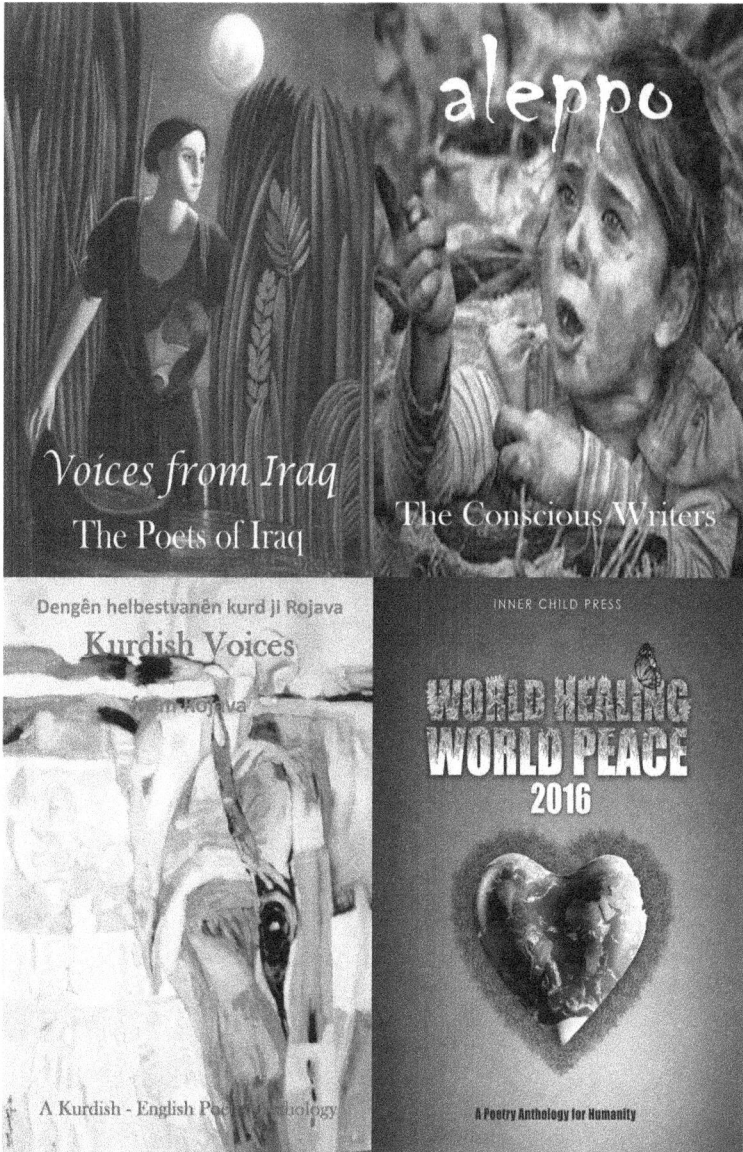

Now Available

www.innerchildpress.com/anthologies

Now Available

www.innerchildpress.com/anthologies

Now Available

www.innerchildpress.com/anthologies

Now Available

www.innerchildpress.com/anthologies

The Year of the Poet
January 2014

The Poetry Posse

Jamie Bond
Gail Weston Shazor
Albert 'Infinite' Carrasco
Siddartha Beth Pierce
Janet P. Caldwell
June 'Bugg' Barefield
Debbie M. Allen
Tony Henninger
Joe DaVerbal Minddancer
Robert Gibbons
Neetu Wali
Shareef Abdur-Rasheed
William S. Peters, Sr.

Carnation

Our January Feature
Terri L. Johnson

the Year of the Poet
February 2014

violets

The Poetry Posse

Jamie Bond
Gail Weston Shazor
Albert 'Infinite' Carrasco
Siddartha Beth Pierce
Janet P. Caldwell
June 'Bugg' Barefield
Debbie M. Allen
Tony Henninger
Joe DaVerbal Minddancer
Robert Gibbons
Neetu Wali
Shareef Abdur-Rasheed
William S. Peters, Sr.

Our February Features
Teresa E. Gallion & Robert Gibson

the Year of the Poet
March 2014

The Poetry Posse

Jamie Bond
Gail Weston Shazor
Albert 'Infinite' Carrasco
Siddartha Beth Pierce
Janet P. Caldwell
June 'Bugg' Barefield
Debbie M. Allen
Tony Henninger
Joe DaVerbal Minddancer
Robert Gibbons
Neetu Wali
Shareef Abdur-Rasheed
Kimberly Burnham
William S. Peters, Sr.

daffodils

Our March Featured Poets
Alicia C. Cooper & hülya yılmaz

the Year of the Poet
April 2014

The Poetry Posse

Jamie Bond
Gail Weston Shazor
Albert 'Infinite' Carrasco
Siddartha Beth Pierce
Janet P. Caldwell
June 'Bugg' Barefield
Debbie M. Allen
Tony Henninger
Joe DaVerbal Minddancer
Robert Gibbons
Neetu Wali
Shareef Abdur-Rasheed
Kimberly Burnham
William S. Peters, Sr.

Our April Featured Poets
Fahredin Shehu
Martina Reisz Newberry
Justin Blackburn
Monte Smith

Sweet Pea

celebrating international poetry month

Now Available

www.innerchildpress.com/the-year-of-the-poet

the year of the poet
May 2014

May's Featured Poets

ReeCee
Joski the Poet
Shannon Stanton

Dedicated To our Children

The Poetry Posse

Jamie Bond
Gail Weston Shazor
Albert Infinite Carrasco
Siddartha Beth Pierce
Janet P. Caldwell
June 'Bugg' Barefield
Debbie M. Allen
Tony Henninger
Joe DaVerbal Minddancer
Robert Gibbons
Neetu Wali
Shameef Abdur-Rasheed
Kimberly Burnham
William S. Peters, Sr.

Lily of the Valley

the Year of the Poet
June 2014

Love & Relationship

Rose

June's Featured Poets

Shantelle McLin
Jacqueline D. E. Kennedy
Abraham N. Benjamin

The Poetry Posse

Jamie Bond
Gail Weston Shazor
Albert Infinite Carrasco
Siddartha Beth Pierce
Janet P. Caldwell
June Bugg Barefield
Debbie M. Allen
Tony Henninger
Joe DaVerbal Minddancer
Robert Gibbons
Neetu Wali
Shareef Abdur-Rasheed
Kimberly Burnham
William S. Peters, Sr.

The Year of the Poet
July 2014

July Feature Poets

Christena A. V. Williams
Dru-Sonn R. Scrum
Rolade Otanrewaju Freedom

The Poetry Posse

Jamie Bond
Gail Weston Shazor
Albert Infinite Carrasco
Siddartha Beth Pierce
Janet P. Caldwell
June 'Bugg' Barefield
Debbie M. Allen
Tony Henninger
Joe DaVerbal Minddancer
Robert Gibbons
Neetu Wali
Shareef Abdur-Rasheed
Kimberly Burnham
William S. Peters, Sr.

Lotus
Asian Flower of the Month

The Year of the Poet
August 2014

Gladiolus

The Poetry Posse

Jamie Bond
Gail Weston Shazor
Albert Infinite Carrasco
Siddartha Beth Pierce
Janet P. Caldwell
June 'Bugg' Barefield
Debbie M. Allen
Tony Henninger
Joe DaVerbal Minddancer
Robert Gibbons
Neetu Wali
Shareef Abdur-Rasheed
Kimberly Burnham
William S. Peters, Sr.

August Feature Poets

Ann White * Rosalind Cherry * Shelia Jenkins

Now Available

www.innerchildpress.com/the-year-of-the-poet

The Year of the Poet

September 2014

Aster   Morning-Glory

Wild Child of September Birthday Flower

September Feature Poets
Florence Malone * Keith Alan Hamilton

The Poetry Posse
Jamie Bond * Gail Weston Shazor * Albert 'Infinite' Carrasco * Siddartha Beth Pierce
Janet P. Caldwell * June 'Bugg' Barefield * Debbie M. Allen * Tony Henninger
Joe DaVerbal Minddancer * Robert Gibbons * Neetu Wali * Shareef Abdur-Rasheed
Kimberly Burnham * William S. Peters, Sr.

THE YEAR OF THE POET

October 2014

Red Poppy

The Poetry Posse
Jamie Bond * Gail Weston Shazor * Albert 'Infinite' Carrasco * Siddartha Beth Pierce
Janet P. Caldwell * June 'Bugg' Barefield * Debbie M. Allen * Tony Henninger
Joe DaVerbal Minddancer * Robert Gibbons * Neetu Wali * Shareef Abdur-Rasheed
Kimberly Burnham * William S. Peters, Sr.

October Feature Poets
Ceri Naz * Rajendra Padhi * Elizabeth Castillo

THE YEAR OF THE POET

November 2014

Chrysanthemum

The Poetry Posse
Jamie Bond * Gail Weston Shazor * Albert 'Infinite' Carrasco * Siddartha Beth Pierce
Janet P. Caldwell * June 'Bugg' Barefield * Debbie M. Allen * Tony Henninger
Joe DaVerbal Minddancer * Robert Gibbons * Neetu Wali * Shareef Abdur-Rasheed
Kimberly Burnham * William S. Peters, Sr.

November Feature Poets
Jocelyn Mosman * Jackie Allen * James Moore * Neville Hiatt

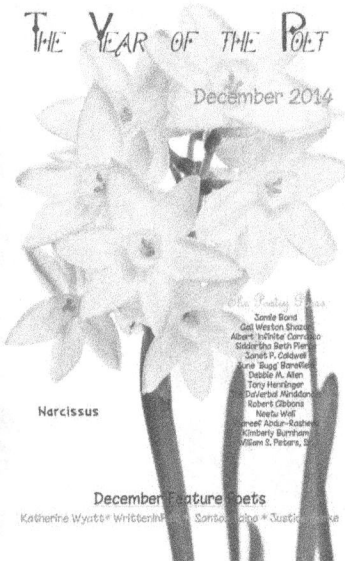

THE YEAR OF THE POET

December 2014

The Poetry Posse
Jamie Bond
Gail Weston Shazor
Albert 'Infinite' Carrasco
Siddartha Beth Pierce
Janet P. Caldwell
June 'Bugg' Barefield
Debbie M. Allen
Tony Henninger
DaVerbal Minddancer
Robert Gibbons
Neetu Wali
Shareef Abdur-Rasheed
Kimberly Burnham
William S. Peters, Sr.

Narcissus

December Feature Poets
Katherine Wyatt * WrittenInk... * Santok Saina * Justin... ...

Now Available

www.innerchildpress.com/the-year-of-the-poet

THE YEAR OF THE POET II
January 2015

Garnet

The Poetry Posse
Jamie Bond
Gail Weston Shazor
Albert 'Infinite' Carrasco
Siddartha Beth Pierce
Janet P. Caldwell
Tony Henninger
Joe DaVerbal Minddancer
Robert Gibbons
Neetu Wali
Shareef Abdur – Rasheed
Ann White
Keith Alan Hamilton
Katherine Wyatt
Fahredin Shehu
Hülya N. Yilmaz
Teresa E. Gallion
Jackie Allen
William S. Peters, Sr.

January Feature Poets
Bismay Mohanti * Jen Walls * Eric Judah

THE YEAR OF THE POET II
February 2015

Amethyst

THE POETRY POSSE
Jamie Bond
Gail Weston Shazor
Albert 'Infinite' Carrasco
Siddartha Beth Pierce
Janet P. Caldwell
Tony Henninger
Joe DaVerbal Minddancer
Robert Gibbons
Neetu Wali
Shareef Abdur – Rasheed
Kimberly Burnham
Ann White
Keith Alan Hamilton
Katherine Wyatt
Fahredin Shehu
N. Yilmaz
E. Gallion
Jackie Allen
m S. Peters, Sr.

FEBRUARY FEATURE POETS
Iram Fatima * Bob McNeil * Kerstin Centervall

The Year of the Poet II
March 2015

Our Featured Poets
Heung Sook * Anthony Arnold * Alicia Poland

Bloodstone

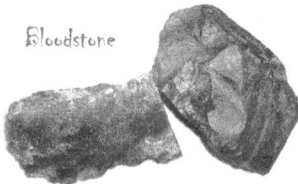

The Poetry Posse 2015
Jamie Bond * Gail Weston Shazor * Albert 'Infinite' Carrasco
Siddartha Beth Pierce * Janet P. Caldwell * Tony Henninger
Joe DaVerbal Minddancer * Neetu Wali * Shareef Abdur – Rasheed
Kimberly Burnham * Ann White * Keith Alan Hamilton
Katherine Wyatt * Fahredin Shehu * Hülya N. Yilmaz
Teresa E. Gallion * Jackie Allen * William S. Peters, Sr

The Year of the Poet II
April 2015

Celebrating International Poetry Month

Our Featured Poets
Raja Williams * Dennis Ferado * Laure Charazac

Diamonds

The Poetry Posse 2015
Jamie Bond * Gail Weston Shazor * Albert 'Infinite' Carrasco
Siddartha Beth Pierce * Janet P. Caldwell * Tony Henninger
Joe DaVerbal Minddancer * Neetu Wali * Shareef Abdur – Rasheed
Kimberly Burnham * Ann White * Keith Alan Hamilton
Katherine Wyatt * Fahredin Shehu * Hülya N. Yilmaz
Teresa E. Gallion * Jackie Allen * William S. Peters, Sr

Now Available

www.innerchildpress.com/the-year-of-the-poet

The Year of the Poet II
May 2015

May's Featured Poets

Geri Algeri
Akin Mosi Chinnery
Anna Jakubcza

Emeralds

The Poetry Posse 2015

Jamie Bond * Gail Weston Shazor * Albert 'Infinite' Carrasco
Siddartha Beth Pierce * Janet P. Caldwell * Tony Henninger
Joe DaVerbal Minddancer * Neetu Wali * Shareef Abdur – Rasheed
Kimberly Burnham * Ann White * Keith Alan Hamilton
Katherine Wyatt * Fahredin Shehu * Hülya N. Yılmaz
Teresa E. Gallion * Jackie Allen * William S. Peters. Sr.

The Year of the Poet II
June 2015

June's Featured Poets

Amihit Arustamyan * Yvette D. Murrell * Regina A. Walker

Pearl

The Poetry Posse 2015

Jamie Bond * Gail Weston Shazor * Albert 'Infinite' Carrasco
Siddartha Beth Pierce * Janet P. Caldwell * Tony Henninger
Joe DaVerbal Minddancer * Neetu Wali * Shareef Abdur – Rasheed
Kimberly Burnham * Ann White * Keith Alan Hamilton
Katherine Wyatt * Fahredin Shehu * Hülya N. Yılmaz
Teresa E. Gallion * Jackie Allen * William S. Peters. Sr.

The Year of the Poet II
July 2015

The Featured Poets for July 2015
Abhik Shome * Christina Neal * Robert Neal

Rubies

The Poetry Posse 2015

Jamie Bond * Gail Weston Shazor * Albert 'Infinite' Carrasco
Siddartha Beth Pierce * Janet P. Caldwell * Tony Henninger
Joe DaVerbal Minddancer * Neetu Wali * Shareef Abdur – Rasheed
Kimberly Burnham * Ann White * Keith Alan Hamilton
Katherine Wyatt * Fahredin Shehu * Hülya N. Yılmaz
Teresa E. Gallion * Jackie Allen * William S. Peters. Sr.

The Year of the Poet II
August 2015

Peridot

Featured Poets

Gayle Howell
Ann Chalasz
Christopher Schultz

The Poetry Posse 2015

Jamie Bond * Gail Weston Shazor * Albert 'Infinite' Carrasco
Siddartha Beth Pierce * Janet P. Caldwell * Tony Henninger
Joe DaVerbal Minddancer * Neetu Wali * Shareef Abdur – Rasheed
Kimberly Burnham * Ann White * Keith Alan Hamilton
Katherine Wyatt * Fahredin Shehu * Hülya N. Yılmaz
Teresa E. Gallion * Jackie Allen * William S. Peters. Sr.

Now Available

www.innerchildpress.com/the-year-of-the-poet

The Year of the Poet II
September 2015

Featured Poets
Alfreda Ghee   Lonneice Weeks Badley   Demetrios Trifiatis

Sapphires

The Poetry Posse 2015

Jamie Bond * Gail Weston Shazor * Albert 'Infinite' Carrasco
Siddartha Beth Pierce * Janet P. Caldwell * Tony Henninger
Joe DaVerbal Minddancer * Neetu Wali * Shareef Abdur – Rasheed
Kimberly Burnham * Ann White * Keith Alan Hamilton
Katherine Wyatt * Fahredin Shehu * Hülya N. Yılmaz
Teresa E. Gallion * Jackie Allen * William S. Peters, Sr.

The Year of the Poet II
October 2015

Featured Poets
Monte Smith * Laura J. Wolfe * William Washington

Opal

The Poetry Posse 2015

Jamie Bond * Gail Weston Shazor * Albert 'Infinite' Carrasco
Siddartha Beth Pierce * Janet P. Caldwell * Tony Henninger
Joe DaVerbal Minddancer * Neetu Wali * Shareef Abdur – Rasheed
Kimberly Burnham * Ann White * Keith Alan Hamilton
Katherine Wyatt * Fahredin Shehu * Hülya N. Yılmaz
Teresa E. Gallion * Jackie Allen * William S. Peters, Sr.

The Year of the Poet II
November 2015

Featured Poets
Alan W. Jankowski
Bismay Mohanty
James Moore

Topaz

The Poetry Posse 2015

Jamie Bond * Gail Weston Shazor * Albert 'Infinite' Carrasco
Siddartha Beth Pierce * Janet P. Caldwell * Tony Henninger
Joe DaVerbal Minddancer * Neetu Wali * Shareef Abdur – Rasheed
Kimberly Burnham * Ann White * Keith Alan Hamilton
Katherine Wyatt * Fahredin Shehu * Hülya N. Yılmaz
Teresa E. Gallion * Jackie Allen * William S. Peters, Sr.

The Year of the Poet II
December 2015

Featured Poets
Kerione Bryan * Michelle Joan Barulich * Neville Hiatt

Turquoise

The Poetry Posse 2015

Jamie Bond * Gail Weston Shazor * Albert 'Infinite' Carrasco
Siddartha Beth Pierce * Janet P. Caldwell * Tony Henninger
Joe DaVerbal Minddancer * Neetu Wali * Shareef Abdur – Rasheed
Kimberly Burnham * Ann White * Keith Alan Hamilton
Katherine Wyatt * Fahredin Shehu * Hülya N. Yılmaz
Teresa E. Gallion * Jackie Allen * William S. Peters, Sr.

Now Available

www.innerchildpress.com/the-year-of-the-poet

Now Available

www.innerchildpress.com/the-year-of-the-poet

The Year of the Poet
May 2016

Bob Strum
Barbara Allan
D.L. Davis

Oriole

The Year of the Poet III
June 2016

Featured Poets

Qibrije Demiri- Frangu
Naime Beqiraj
Faleeha Hassan
Bedri Zyberaj

Black Necked Stilt

The Poetry Posse 2016

The Year of the Poet
July 2016

Iram Fatima 'Ashi'
Langley Shazor
Jody Doty
Emilia T. Davis

Indigo Bunting

The Poetry Posse 2016

The Year of the Poet III
August 2016

Featured Poets

Anita Dash
Irena Jovanovic
Malgorzata Gouluda

Painted Bunting

The Poetry Posse 2016

Now Available

www.innerchildpress.com/the-year-of-the-poet

The Year of the Poet III
September 2016

Featured Poets

Simone Weber
Abhijit Sen
Eunice Barbara C. Novio

Long Billed Curle

The Poetry Posse 2016

The Year of the Poet III
October 2016

Featured Poets

Lara Joseph
Uma Krishnamurthy R
James Moore

Barn Owl

The Poetry Posse 2016

The Year of the Poet III
November 2016

Featured Poets

Rosemary Burns
Robin Ouzman Hislop
Lonneice Weeks-Badler

Northern Cardinal

The Poetry Posse 2016

The Year of the Poet III
December 2016

Featured Poets

Samih Masoud
Mountassir Aziz Bien
Abdulkadir Musa

Rough Legged Hawk

The Poetry Posse 2016

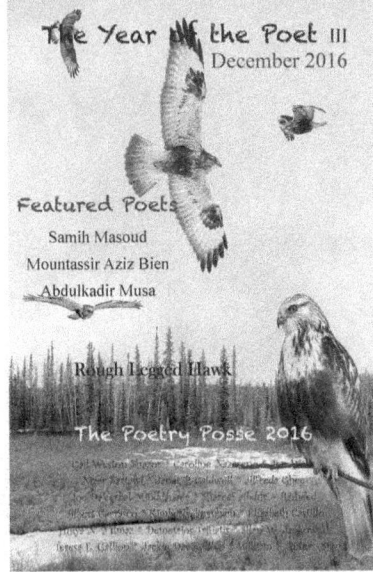

Now Available

www.innerchildpress.com/the-year-of-the-poet

The Year of the Poet IV — January 2017

The Year of the Poet IV — February 2017

The Year of the Poet IV — March 2017

The Year of the Poet IV — April 2017

Now Available

www.innerchildpress.com/the-year-of-the-poet

The Year of the Poet IV
May 2017

The Flowering Dogwood Tree

Featured Poets
Kallisa Powell
Alicja Maria Kuberska
Fethi Sassi

The Poetry Posse 2017

Gil Weston Shazor * Caroline Nazareno * Bismay Mohanty
Teresa E. Gallion * Anna Jakubczak Vel Ratty Adalan
Joe DaVerbal Minddancer * Shareef Abdur - Rasheed
Albert Carrasco * Kimberly Burnham * Elizabeth Castillo
Hülya N. Yılmaz * Poleshe Hasson * Jackie Davis Allen
Jen Walls * Nizar Sartawi * * William S. Peters, Sr.

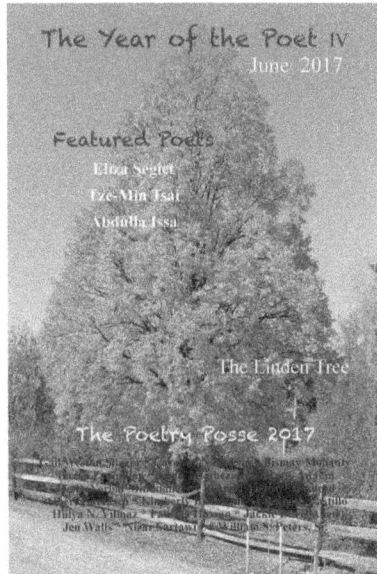

The Year of the Poet IV
June 2017

Featured Poets
Eliza Segiet
Eze-Min Tsai
Abdulla Issa

The Linden Tree

The Poetry Posse 2017

Hülya N. Yılmaz * Bismay Mohanty
Jen Walls * Nizar Sartawi * * William S. Peters

The Year of the Poet IV
July 2017

Featured Poets
Anca Mihaela Bruma
Ibaa Ismail
Zvonko Taneski

The Oak Moon

The Poetry Posse 2017

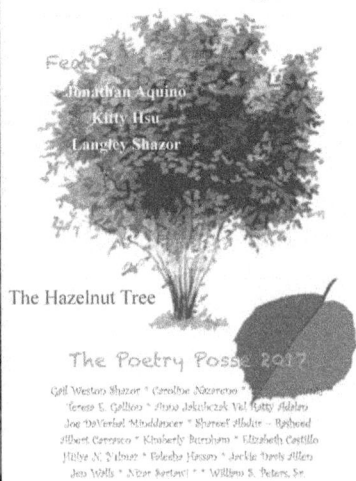

The Year of the Poet IV
August 2017

Featured Poets
Jonathan Aquino
Kitty Hsu
Langley Shazor

The Hazelnut Tree

The Poetry Posse 2017

Gil Weston Shazor * Caroline Nazareno *
Teresa E. Gallion * Anna Jakubczak Vel Ratty Adalan
Joe DaVerbal Minddancer * Shareef Abdur – Rasheed
Albert Carrasco * Kimberly Burnham * Elizabeth Castillo
Hülya N. Yılmaz * Poleshe Hasson * Jackie Davis Allen
Jen Walls * Nizar Sartawi * * William S. Peters, Sr.

Now Available

www.innerchildpress.com/the-year-of-the-poet

The Year of the Poet IV
September 2017

Featured Poets

Martina Reisz Newberry
Ameer Nassir
Christine Fulco Neal
Robert Neal

The Elm Tree

The Poetry Posse 2017

Gail Weston Shazor * Caroline Nazareno * Bismay Mohanty
Teresa E. Gallion * Anna Jakubczak Vel Ratty Adalan
Joe DaVerbal Minddancer * Shareef Abdur – Rasheed
Albert Carrasco * Kimberly Burnham * Elizabeth Castillo
Hülya N. Yılmaz * Faleeha Hassan * Jackie Davis Allen
Jen Walls * Nizar Sartawi * * William S. Peters, Sr.

The Year of the Poet IV
October 2017

Featured Poets

Ahmed Abu Saleem
Nedal Al-Qaeim
Sadeddin Shahin

The Black Walnut Tree

The Poetry Posse 2017

Gail Weston Shazor * Caroline Nazareno * Bismay Mohanty
Teresa E. Gallion * Anna Jakubczak Vel Ratty Adalan
Joe DaVerbal Minddancer * Shareef Abdur – Rasheed
Albert Carrasco * Kimberly Burnham * Elizabeth Castillo
Hülya N. Yılmaz * Faleeha Hassan * Jackie Davis Allen
Jen Walls * Nizar Sartawi * * William S. Peters, Sr.

The Year of the Poet IV
November 2017

Featured Poets

Kay Peters
Alfreda D. Ghee
Gabriella Garofalo
Rosemary Cappello

The Tree of Life

The Poetry Posse 2017

Gail Weston Shazor * Caroline Nazareno * Bismay Mohanty
Teresa E. Gallion * Anna Jakubczak Vel Ratty Adalan
Joe DaVerbal Minddancer * Shareef Abdur – Rasheed
Albert Carrasco * Kimberly Burnham * Elizabeth Castillo
Hülya N. Yılmaz * Faleeha Hassan * Jackie Davis Allen
Jen Walls * Nizar Sartawi * William S. Peters, Sr.

The Year of the Poet IV
December 2017

Featured Poets

Justice Clarke
Mariel M. Pabroa
Kiley Brown

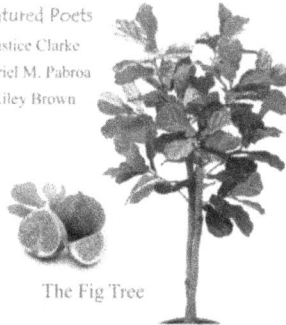

The Fig Tree

The Poetry Posse 2017

Gail Weston Shazor * Caroline Nazareno * Bismay Mohanty
Teresa E. Gallion * Anna Jakubczak Vel Ratty Adalan
Joe DaVerbal Minddancer * Shareef Abdur – Rasheed
Albert Carrasco * Kimberly Burnham * Elizabeth Castillo
Hülya N. Yılmaz * Faleeha Hassan * Jackie Davis Allen
Jen Walls * Nizar Sartawi * William S. Peters, Sr.

Now Available

www.innerchildpress.com/the-year-of-the-poet

The Year of the Poet V
January 2018

Featured Poets

Iyad Shamasnah

Yasmeen Hamzeh

Ali Abdolrezaei

Aksum

The Poetry Posse 2018

Gail Weston Shazor * Caroline Nazareno * Tezmin Ition Tsai
Hülya N. Yilmaz * Faleeha Hassan * Jackie Davis Allen
Teresa E. Gallion * Anna Jakubczak Vel Ratty Adalan
Alicja Maria Kuberska * Shareef Abdur - Rasheed
Kimberly Burnham * Elizabeth Castillo
Nizar Sartawi * William S. Peters, Sr.

The Year of the Poet V
February 2018

Sabean

Featured Poets

Muhammad Azram

Anna Szawracka

Abhilipsa Kuanar

Aanika Aory

The Poetry Posse 2018

Gail Weston Shazor * Caroline Nazareno * Tezmin Ition Tsai
Hülya N. Yilmaz * Faleeha Hassan * Jackie Davis Allen
Teresa E. Gallion * Anna Jakubczak Vel Ratty Adalan
Alicja Maria Kuberska * Shareef Abdur - Rasheed
Kimberly Burnham * Elizabeth Castillo
Nizar Sartawi * William S. Peters, Sr.

The Year of the Poet V
March 2018

Featured Poets

Irum Fatima 'Aashi'
Cassandra Swan
Jaleel Khazaal
Shazia Zaman

Mexico   Cuba

Dominican
Republic

Belize   Haiti
Guatemala Honduras Jamaica   Puerto Rico
El Salvador   Nicaragua
Costa Rica   Panama

Caribbean
&
Middle America

Colombia

The Poetry Posse 2018

Gail Weston Shazor * Nizar Sartawi * Hülya N. Yilmaz
Jackie Davis Allen * Caroline 'Ceri' Nazareno
Alicja Maria Kuberska * Teresa E. Gallion
Faleeha Hassan * Shareef Abdur - Rasheed
Kimberly Burnham * Elizabeth Castillo
Tezmin Ition Tsai * William S. Peters, Sr.

The Year of the Poet V
April 2018

Featured Poets

The Nez Perce

The Poetry Posse 2018

Now Available

www.innerchildpress.com/the-year-of-the-poet

The Year of the Poet V
May 2018

Featured Poets

The Sumerians

The Poetry Posse 2018

Gail Weston Shazor * Nizar Sartawi * Hülya N. Yılmaz
Jackie Davis Allen * Caroline 'Ceri' Nazareno
Alicja Maria Kubenska * Teresa E. Gallion
Kimberly Burnham * Shareef Abdur – Rasheed
Faleeha Hassan * Elizabeth Castillo * Swapna Behera
Tezmin Ition Tsai * William S. Peters, Sr.

The Year of the Poet V
June 2018

Featured Poets

Bdbil Mahqi * Daim Miftari * Gjoko Bozovic * Sofija Živkova

The Paleo Indians

The Poetry Posse 2018

The Year of the Poet V
July 2018

Featured Poets

Pedmola Irengat-Paddy
Mohammad Ikbal Hardi
Eliza Segiet
Tom Higgins

Oceania

The Poetry Posse 2018

The Year of the Poet V
August 2018

Featured Poets
Hussein Habasch * Mircea Dan Duta * Naida Mujkić * Swagat Das

The Lapita

The Poetry Posse 2018

Gail Weston Shazor * Nizar Sartawi * Hülya N. Yılmaz
Jackie Davis Allen * Caroline 'Ceri' Nazareno
Alicja Maria Kubenska * Teresa E. Gallion
Kimberly Burnham * Shareef Abdur – Rasheed
Ashok K. Bhargava* Elizabeth Castillo * Swapna Behaera
Tezmin Ition Tsai * William S. Peters, Sr.

Now Available

www.innerchildpress.com/the-year-of-the-poet

The Year of the Poet V
September 2018

The Aztecs & Incas

Featured Poets
Kolade Olanrewaju Freedom
Eliza Segiet
Mazhar Hussain Abdul Ghani
Lily Swarn

The Poetry Posse 2018

Gail Weston Shazor * Nizar Sartawi * Hülya N. Yılmaz
Jackie Davis Allen * Caroline 'Ceri' Nazareno
Alicja Maria Kubenska * Teresa E. Gallion
Kimberly Burnham * Shareef Abdur – Rasheed
Ashok K. Bhargava * Elizabeth Castillo * Swapna Behaera
Tezmin Ition Tsai * William S. Peters, Sr.

The Year of the Poet V
October 2018

Featured Poets
Alicia Minjarez * Lonnice Weeks-Badley
Lopamudra Mishra * Abdelwahed Souayah

Bengali

The Poetry Posse 2018

Gail Weston Shazor * Nizar Sartawi * Hülya N. Yılmaz
Jackie Davis Allen * Caroline 'Ceri' Nazareno
Alicja Maria Kubenska * Teresa E. Gallion
Kimberly Burnham * Shareef Abdur – Rasheed
Ashok K. Bhargava * Elizabeth Castillo * Swapna Behaera
Tezmin Ition Tsai * William S. Peters, Sr.

The Year of the Poet V
November 2018

Featured Poets
Michelle Joan Barufich * Monsif Beroual
Krystyna Konecka * Nassira Nezzar

The Poetry Posse 2018

Gail Weston Shazor * Nizar Sartawi * Hülya N. Yılmaz
Jackie Davis Allen * Caroline 'Ceri' Nazareno
Alicja Maria Kubenska * Teresa E. Gallion
Kimberly Burnham * Shareef Abdur – Rasheed
Ashok K. Bhargava * Elizabeth Castillo * Swapna Behera
Tezmin Ition Tsai * William S. Peters, Sr.

The Year of the Poet V
December 2018

Featured Poets
Rose Terranova Cirigliano
Joanna Kalinowska
Sokolović Emin
Dr. T. Ashok Chakravarthy

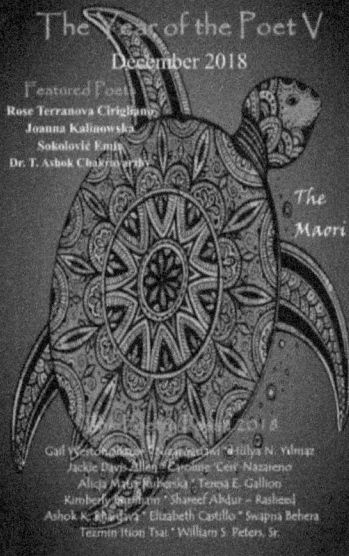

The
Maori

The Poetry Posse 2018

Gail Weston Shazor * Nizar Sartawi * Hülya N. Yılmaz
Jackie Davis Allen * Caroline 'Ceri' Nazareno
Alicja Maria Kubenska * Teresa E. Gallion
Kimberly Burnham * Shareef Abdur – Rasheed
Ashok K. Bhargava * Elizabeth Castillo * Swapna Behera
Tezmin Ition Tsai * William S. Peters, Sr.

Now Available

www.innerchildpress.com/the-year-of-the-poet

The Year of the Poet VI

January 2019

Indigenous North Americans

Featured Poets

Houda Elfchiali
Anthony Briseve
Iran Fatima 'Ashi'
Dr. K. K. Mathew

Dream Catcher

The Poetry Posse 2019

Gail Weston Shazor * Joe Paire * Hülya N. Yılmaz
Jackie Davis Allen * Caroline Nazareno
Alicja Maria Kuberska * Teresa E. Gallion
Kimberly Burnham * Shareef Abdur - Rasheed
Ashok K. Bhargava * Elizabeth Castillo * Swapna Behera
Tezmin Ition Tsai * William S. Peters, Sr.

The Year of the Poet VI

February 2019

Featured Poets

Marek Lukaszewier * Bharati Nayak
Aida G. Roque * Jean-Jacques Fournier

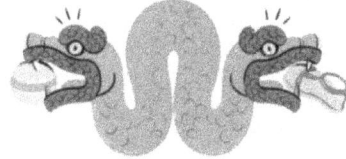

Meso-America

The Poetry Posse 2019

Gail Weston Shazor * Albert Carrasco * Hülya N. Yılmaz
Jackie Davis Allen * Caroline Nazareno * Eliza Segiet
Alicja Maria Kuberska * Teresa E. Gallion * Joe Paire
Kimberly Burnham * Shareef Abdur - Rasheed
Ashok K. Bhargava * Elizabeth Castillo * Swapna Behera
Tezmin Ition Tsai * William S. Peters, Sr.

The Year of the Poet VI

March 2019

Featured Poets

Eness Mahmud * Sylwia K. Malinowska
Shurouk Hammoud * Anwer Ghani

The Caribbean

The Poetry Posse 2019

Gail Weston Shazor * Albert Carrasco * Hülya N. Yılmaz
Jackie Davis Allen * Caroline Nazareno * Eliza Segiet
Alicja Maria Kuberska * Teresa E. Gallion * Joe Paire
Kimberly Burnham * Shareef Abdur - Rasheed
Ashok K. Bhargava * Elizabeth Castillo * Swapna Behera
Tezmin Ition Tsai * William S. Peters, Sr.

The Year of the Poet VI

April 2019

Featured Poets

DL Davis * Michelle Joan Barulich
Lulëzim Haziri * Faleeha Hassan

Central & West Africa

The Poetry Posse 2019

Gail Weston Shazor * Albert Carrasco * Hülya N. Yılmaz
Jackie Davis Allen * Caroline Nazareno * Eliza Segiet
Alicja Maria Kuberska * Teresa E. Gallion * Joe Paire
Kimberly Burnham * Shareef Abdur - Rasheed
Ashok K. Bhargava * Elizabeth Castillo * Swapna Behera
Tezmin Ition Tsai * William S. Peters, Sr.

Now Available

www.innerchildpress.com/the-year-of-the-poet

The Year of the Poet VI
May 2019

Featured Poets

Emad Al-Haydary * Hussein Nasser Jabr
Wahab Sheriff * Abdul Razzaq Al Ameeri

Asia Southeast Asia and Maritime Asia

The Poetry Posse 2019

Gail Weston Shazor * Albert Carrasco * Hülya N. Yılmaz
Jackie Davis Allen * Caroline Nazareno * Eliza Segiet
Alicja Maria Kuberska * Teresa E. Gallion * Joe Paire
Kimberly Burnham * Shareef Abdur – Rasheed
Ashok K. Bhargava * Elizabeth Castillo * Swapna Behera
Tezmin Ition Tsai * William S. Peters, Sr.

The Year of the Poet VI
June 2019

Featured Poets

Kate Gaudi Powiekszone * Sahaj Sabharwal
Iwu Jeff * Mohamed Abdel Aziz Shmeis

Arctic
Circumpolar

The Poetry Posse 2019

Gail Weston Shazor * Albert Carrasco * Hülya N. Yılmaz
Jackie Davis Allen * Caroline Nazareno * Eliza Segiet
Alicja Maria Kuberska * Teresa E. Gallion * Joe Paire
Kimberly Burnham * Shareef Abdur – Rasheed
Ashok K. Bhargava * Elizabeth Castillo * Swapna Behera
Tezmin Ition Tsai * William S. Peters, Sr.

The Year of the Poet VI

Featured Poets

Saadeddin Shahia * Andy Scott
Fahredin Shehu * Alok Kumar Ray

The Horn of Africa

Ethiopia   Djibouti

Somalia   Eritrea

The Poetry Posse 2019

Gail Weston Shazor * Albert Carrasco * Hülya N. Yılmaz
Jackie Davis Allen * Caroline Nazareno * Eliza Segiet
Alicja Maria Kuberska * Teresa E. Gallion * Joe Paire
Kimberly Burnham * Shareef Abdur – Rasheed
Ashok K. Bhargava * Elizabeth Castillo * Swapna Behera
Tezmin Ition Tsai * William S. Peters, Sr.

The Year of the Poet VI
August 2019

Featured Poets

Shola Balogun * Bharati Nayak
Monalisa Dash Dwibedy * Mbizo Chirasha

Coexist

Southwest Asia

The Poetry Posse 2019

Gail Weston Shazor * Albert Carrasco * Hülya N. Yılmaz
Jackie Davis Allen * Caroline Nazareno * Eliza Segiet
Alicja Maria Kuberska * Teresa E. Gallion * Joe Paire
Kimberly Burnham * Shareef Abdur – Rasheed
Ashok K. Bhargava * Elizabeth Castillo * Swapna Behera
Tezmin Ition Tsai * William S. Peters, Sr.

Now Available

www.innerchildpress.com/the-year-of-the-poet

and there is much, much more !

visit . . .

www.innerchildpress.com/antho logies-sales-special.php

Also check out our Authors and all the wonderful Books Available at :

www.innerchildpress.com/autho rs-pages

INNER CHILD PRESS

WORLD HEALING WORLD PEACE
2018

A Poetry Anthology for Humanity

Now Available

www.worldhealingworldpeacepoetry.com

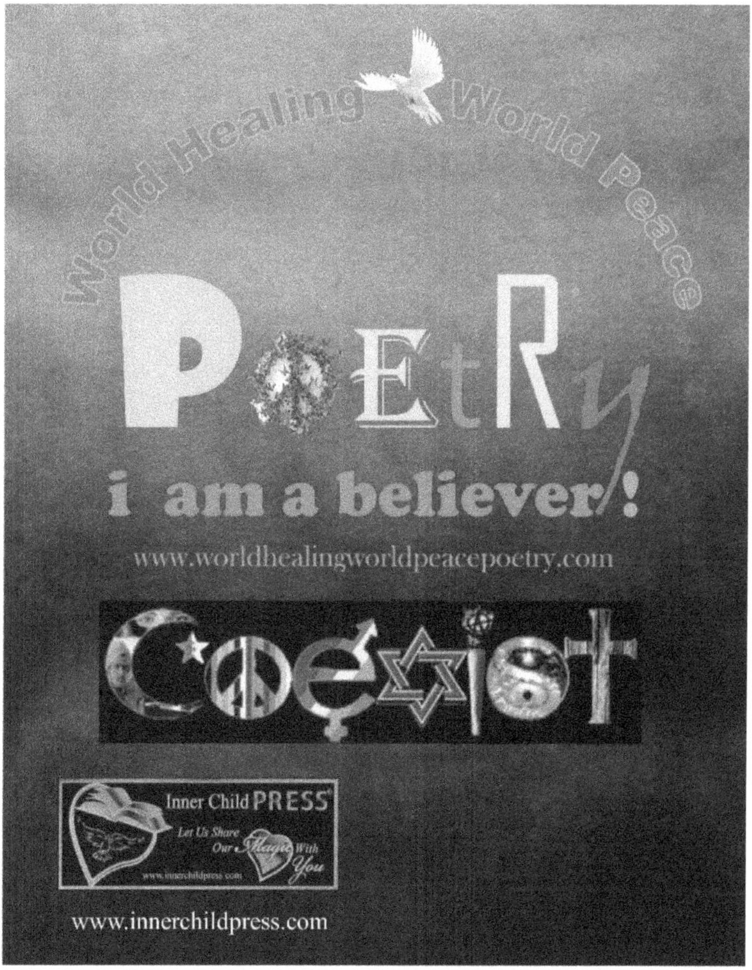

Now Available

www.worldhealingworldpeacepoetry.com

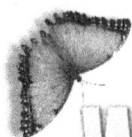

World Healing
World Peace

support

www.worldhealingworldpeacepoetry.com

World Healing
World Peace
2018

Now Available

www.worldhealingworldpeacepoetry.com

Inner Child Press International

'building bridges of cultural understanding'

Meet the Board of Directors

www.innerchildpress.com

Inner Child Press International

'building bridges of cultural understanding'

Meet our Cultural Ambassadors

Fahredin Shehu
Director of Cultural

Faleha Hassan
Iraq – USA

Elizabeth E. Castillo
Philippines

Antoinette Coleman
Chicago
Midwest USA

Ananda Nepali
Nepal – USA
Southern Asia

Kimberly Burnham
Pacific Southwest
USA

Alicja Kuberska
Poland
Eastern Europe

Swapna Behera
India
Southeast Asia

Kolade O. Freedom
Nigeria
West Africa

Monsif Beroual
Morocco
Northern Africa

Ashok K. Bhargava
Canada

Tzemin Ition Tsai
Republic of China
Greater China

Alicia M. Ramírez
Mexico
Central America

Christena AV Williams
Jamaica
Caribbean

Louise Hudon
Eastern Canada

Aziz Mountassir
Morocco
Northern Africa

Shareef Abdur-Rasheed
Southeastern USA

Laure Charazac
France
Western Europe

Mohammad Ikbal Harb
Lebanon
Middle East

Mohamed Abdel Aziz Shmeis
Egypt
Middle East

Hilary Mainga
Kenya
Central Africa

Josephus R. Johnson
Liberia

www.innerchildpress.com

195

This Anthological Publication
is underwritten solely by

Inner Child Press

Inner Child Press is a Publishing Company
Founded and Operated by Writers. Our
personal publishing experiences provides
us an intimate understanding of the
sometimes daunting challenges Writers,
New and Seasoned may face in the
Business of Publishing and Marketing
their Creative "Written Work".

For more Information

Inner Child Press

www.innerchildpress.com

'building bridges of cultural understanding'
202 Wiltree Court, State College, Pennsylvania 16801

www.innerchildpress.com

196

~ *fini* ~

Coming
April 2020

The
World Healing, World Peace
International Poetry Symposium

Stay Tuned

for more information

intouch@innerchildpress.com

'building bridges of cultural understanding'

www.innerchildpress.com

www.ingramcontent.com/pod-product-compliance
Lightning Source LLC
LaVergne TN
LVHW011154080426
835508LV00007B/393